The Stoic Father - Parenting in the Face of Adversity- Sensory Processing Disorder

The Stoic Father - Parenting in the Face of Adversity- Sensory Processing Disorder

Deam

CONTENTS

	Introduction	1
one	The Stoic Art of Presence	4
two	Recognizing Sensory Sensitivities in Children	19
three	The Power of Patience	37
four	Emotional Mastery	52
five	Focus on What You Can Control	67
six	Cultivating Gratitude	82
seven	Embracing Change	97
eight	The Power of Reflection	113
nine	The Wisdom of Perspective	129
ten	Embracing Patience	144
	CONCLUSION	170

Introduction

Introduction: A Stoic Approach to Parenting a Child with Sensory Processing Disorder

Raising a child is an extraordinary journey—one that is often filled with joy, challenges, and profound growth. But for parents of children with sensory processing disorder (SPD), the path can be especially complex. Every day can feel like an intricate dance between managing sensory overload, advocating for your child, and maintaining your own well-being. It is a challenge that can often leave you feeling overwhelmed, uncertain, and stretched thin.

As a father of a 6-year-old son with SPD, our son is extraordinary, and adorable and a shining light in my life, but that doesn't mean there hasn't been any difficulties along the way. In fact, there's been more than you could possibly imagine, although, if you're reading this, maybe you can. None the less, I understand these challenges firsthand. I've experienced the frustration of watching my son struggle with sensory sensitivities—whether it's the overwhelming buzz of a crowded room, the irritation of certain fabrics, or the way bright lights can send him into sensory overload. In the face of these daily battles, I found myself searching for ways to stay grounded, to support my son without losing myself in the process, and to find meaning in what often felt like an unrelenting struggle.

Through this search, I turned to Stoic philosophy. Stoicism teaches that while we cannot control the external circumstances in our lives, we have complete control over how we respond. This philosophy offers a perspective that is not just theoretical, but practical—a way to approach life's difficulties with calmness, emotional control, and resilience. The ancient Stoics, such as Marcus Aurelius and Epictetus, teach us that hardship is an inevitable part of life, but that we have the power to control our reactions, our emotions, and our inner peace.

This book is about integrating these timeless Stoic principles with the modern reality of raising a child with SPD. By combining Stoicism with insights from psychology, we will bridge the gap between philosophical wisdom and the practical advice parents need to navigate the complexities of sensory processing challenges. Through this integration, we'll explore how Stoic wisdom can help you manage sensory overload, reduce stress, and develop the resilience necessary to thrive as both a parent and a person.

The principles we will discuss in the coming chapters—emotional mastery, patience, presence, adaptability—are not just abstract concepts; they are tools that can help you respond more effectively to the daily challenges of raising a child with SPD. Whether you are helping your child cope with overwhelming sounds, textures, or lights, or simply trying to keep calm in the face of frustration, Stoic teachings offer a framework for staying balanced. Alongside these Stoic principles, we'll incorporate psychological insights and practical strategies that can immediately improve the way you interact with your child and manage sensory challenges.

This book is divided into ten chapters, each focusing on a different aspect of Stoic wisdom and how it applies to the experience of raising a child with SPD. Each chapter will begin with a thought-provoking quote from a Stoic philosopher or psychologist to set the stage. We'll explore how these ideas can be translated into real-life parenting practices, with each chapter containing three subheadings focused on practical strategies, exercises, and reflections. Along the way, we'll dive into historical stories, personal accounts, and fables that exemplify the core principles, showing how people in the past have applied similar wisdom to overcome adversity.

As you read, you'll discover how small, intentional changes in your mindset can make a world of difference in your parenting. You will learn to let go of the need for perfection, embrace the present moment, and respond with patience and understanding. And most importantly, you will see how the wisdom of the Stoics can help you raise a child who not only survives the challenges of SPD but thrives in spite of them.

By the end of this book, my hope is that you will feel empowered to approach your child's sensory processing disorder with a sense of peace and clarity—knowing that while you may not control every aspect of their world, you have the power to shape your own response. Through Stoic philosophy, we can find the strength, grace, and wisdom needed to raise our children to be the best versions of themselves—regardless of the challenges they face.

Welcome to this journey of transformation, where Stoicism meets parenting, and wisdom leads the way.

One

The Stoic Art of Presence

"The more we value things outside our control, the less control we have." – **Epictetus**

The Importance of Being Present

Understanding the Present Moment

Being a father is one of my two favorite jobs in life—equal first with being a husband. I love my job; I'm incredibly lucky to do what I do. But nothing compares to being a father and a husband, and yet, my work sometimes takes me away from those roles. With my son now being homeschooled, I have the privilege of being his teacher in the mornings, a role that brings us closer together every day. But it also means that my other job demands more of my time. Often, I find myself working late into the evening, not getting home until after 8pm. It's a rarity when I'm able to say good night to my other two children, let alone have a meaningful evening conversation with my wife.

When I do get home, I try. I make a conscious effort to listen to my four-year-old, we talk about dinosaurs, monster trucks, or how fast he is. I hold my baby girl, who screams for her mom until I put her down, and then, as soon as I do, she screams for me again. Eventually, both kids are off to bed. We eat dinner, and then it's time with my wife—talking about our days, her day at work and what she has planned for the kids she teaches tomorrow, we discuss interesting aspects of my day. When she heads to bed, I take a moment for myself, a scotch in hand, usually watching *Star Trek* with Henry since it's his favorite show. I breathe, take it all in, and reflect. It's been a long day, and I'm the first to admit, I don't always get it right, but I try my best to be present for those small moments my family needs from me.

"Presence isn't defined by the size of the moments; it's in the quiet spaces we occupy together. A father's love is not built on grand gestures, but on the consistency of being there, even in the smallest of moments."
– The Philosophical Dad

I don't think life is about the "big" moments. Sure, I'll endeavor to be there for the big events in my kids' lives, but looking back on my own childhood, it's not the big moments I remember. I remember my father taking time off from work just to take me to the batting cages for a couple of hours. After that, he'd return to work, but it's those simple moments—those small acts of presence—that I carry with me. Those are the memories that have stayed with me, and those are the moments I want my children to remember about me and their childhood.

I think it's the quiet, unassuming moments—the ones that may seem small at the time—that build a lasting foundation of love, connection, and growth. I've learned that being truly present for my family is the greatest gift I can offer. Life isn't about the milestones; it's about the simple joys of shared experiences, the quiet moments of connection, and the knowledge that, even in the smallest of actions, we are giving our children the best of us.

The more we value things outside our control, the less control we have. This principle, as articulated by Epictetus, serves as a cornerstone for the Stoic philosophy that champions the cultivation of presence. In the face of chaos, where sensory overload can overwhelm both parent and child, the art of remaining grounded in the present becomes not just a philosophical pursuit but a necessity for maintaining equanimity.

Understanding the present moment is essential. It is here, in this fleeting instant, where our true power resides. The past, with its regrets and missed opportunities, serves no purpose but to distract us from the actions we can take now. The future, shrouded in uncertainty, can provoke anxiety that paralyzes our ability to respond effectively to the challenges at hand. For those who are parents to children with sensory processing disorder, this understanding is vital. The intensity of sensory challenges can ignite emotional responses that spiral into anxiety and frustration, leading to an unproductive cycle that diminishes our capacity for rational thought.

By anchoring ourselves in the present, we reclaim our agency. We are reminded by Stoic teachings that our focus must reside on the now, a realm where we can choose our reactions and cultivate inner tranquility. In moments of sensory overload or emotional upheaval, taking a breath and grounding ourselves in the present allows for clarity and perspective. We can observe our child's needs without the interference of past disappointments or anxieties about the future.

Practically, this translates to an intentional shift in focus. Instead of anticipating the next sensory trigger or replaying previous episodes, we engage fully with the experiences that are unfolding.

This presence fosters an atmosphere of calm, enabling responses that are patient and understanding. By embracing the present, we not only enhance our own well-being but also create an environment of safety and support for our children amidst their sensory challenges.

Through the lens of Stoicism, being present transcends mere mindfulness; it becomes a powerful practice that empowers us to navigate life's complexities with composure and strength. In the present moment, we find the resilience to confront challenges, the wisdom to respond thoughtfully, and the peace that arises from accepting what is. In doing so, we embody the essence of Stoic calm, demonstrating that even in the midst of chaos, we possess the capacity to remain steadfast and composed.

Sensory Overload and the Need for Presence

Sensory overload presents a formidable challenge for both parents and children, manifesting as an overwhelming barrage of sights, sounds, and textures that can induce a state of disarray. In these moments of chaos, the instinctual response may lean toward panic or frustration, emotions that, while natural, can cloud judgment and inhibit constructive action. Herein lies the wisdom of Stoicism: our true strength resides not in the external stimuli that provoke us but in our capacity to govern our reactions.

The Stoic philosophy invites us to cultivate a deliberate response to the chaos around us. When faced with sensory overload, we possess the ability to create a moment of pause—a sacred interval in which we can breathe deeply and collect our thoughts. This pause is not merely a delay but an opportunity to assert our agency. By recognizing this space between stimulus and response, we empower ourselves to act with intention rather than reflexivity.

For parents, this practice of presence is especially vital. In the throes of a child's sensory overwhelm, taking a moment to center oneself enables a clearer perception of the child's needs. It transforms the interaction from one of reaction to one of understanding and support. By remaining calm and composed, a parent can offer the reassurance that a child requires, fostering a sense of security amidst the tumult. This mindful approach not only alleviates the immediate distress but also models emotional resilience for the child.

In embracing the Stoic tenet that we are the masters of our responses, both parents and children can navigate the challenges of sensory overload with increased grace and harmony. The practice of presence becomes a powerful tool, turning moments of potential chaos into opportunities for connection and growth. Through this lens, the experience of sensory overload can evolve from an overwhelming ordeal into a manageable journey, one where understanding and support become the guiding forces.

Thus, we find that the art of presence, cultivated through the principles of Stoicism, allows us to transform chaos into clarity. In this deliberate stillness, we can confront the barrage of stimuli with a sense of calm resolve. Each moment of chaos becomes an invitation to practice virtue, to embody the resilience that lies within us, and to nurture the bonds of connection in the face of adversity. Embracing this art leads not only to personal growth but also to a nurturing environment where both parent and child can flourish amidst the challenges of the world.

Practical Tips for Cultivating Presence
Some practical techniques for cultivating presence in daily life include:

- **Mindful Breathing**: Focus on deep breathing to center yourself, especially during moments of tension. This technique not only calms the mind but also regulates the nervous system, making it easier to stay present and not get caught up in overwhelming emotions.
- **Grounding Exercises**: When things get overwhelming, try focusing on your senses—what you can see, hear, feel, and smell. This sensory grounding brings attention back to the present moment.
- **Body Awareness**: Check in with your body. Are you tense? Are your shoulders clenched? Release that tension consciously. This physical awareness helps us stay connected to the here and now.
- **Mindful Listening**: When communicating with your child, practice listening intently to them without judgment or interruption. This not only improves connection but also anchors you in the present moment.

Accepting What We Cannot Change
Marcus Aurelius – The Stoic Emperor in the Midst of Chaos

Marcus Aurelius, the Stoic Emperor, faced a world rife with chaos, marked by relentless political strife, warfare, and profound personal loss. In such a tumultuous environment, he exemplified a profound sense of tranquility and resolve. His life illustrated the core Stoic tenet that true dominion does not lie in the control of external circumstances but rather in the mastery of one's own mind. His reflections in Meditations serve as a timeless guide for those seeking stability amidst the storms of life.

The essence of Aurelius's philosophy rests on the acceptance of the uncontrollable nature of the world. He understood that while the events surrounding us may spiral into chaos, we possess the sovereign power to govern our thoughts and actions. This realization becomes particularly significant when we confront personal challenges, such as Sensory Processing Disorder (SPD), where the chaos of sensory overload can feel overwhelming. In such instances, embracing the Stoic principle of acceptance allows us to shift our focus from external turmoil to our internal responses.

In the face of stress and sensory onslaught, adopting a Stoic mindset opens the door to resilience. Instead of succumbing to frustration over factors beyond our control, we find strength in our ability to choose our reactions. This awareness fosters a nurturing environment of patience and understanding, not only for ourselves but also for our children.

Marcus Aurelius's teachings remind us that true strength lies in our capacity to maintain inner peace regardless of external circumstances. By concentrating on our thoughts and actions, we can traverse the complexities of life with a steady heart, transforming adversity into a pathway for growth. In doing so, we embrace the Stoic wisdom that not only encourages acceptance of what lies beyond our control but also empowers us to engage thoughtfully with the world around us. This path leads to a deeper understanding of ourselves and a more profound connection with the inherent resilience that resides within us all.

The Stoic Practice of Letting Go:

Recognizing what we can and cannot control is a fundamental principle for parents navigating the complexities of Sensory Processing Disorder (SPD). The struggle to alter or eliminate the sensory difficulties faced by a child can be a source of deep frustration and anxiety. Yet, it is essential to understand that the sensory experiences themselves are not fully within our grasp. Triggers will arise, and sensory overload may strike unexpectedly. In this reality, acceptance becomes a powerful ally. It does not imply resignation, but rather a clear-eyed acknowledgment of the limits of our influence. We cannot dictate every circumstance our child will encounter, nor can we erase their sensory sensitivities.

What we can do, however, is prepare. By thoughtfully adjusting the environment in which our children operate, we create a buffer against the inevitable challenges. Calming routines can serve as anchors, providing stability in a world that often feels chaotic. Furthermore, equipping our children with effective coping strategies empowers them to navigate their experiences with greater ease. This proactive stance fosters resilience, instilling in them the skills to handle adversity.

Thus, we focus on actionable steps, channeling our energy into what is within our control, while consciously releasing the burdens of what is not. This balance between acceptance and action allows us to move forward with clarity and purpose. It is a path marked by fortitude, where we embrace our role in guiding our children without becoming overwhelmed by what lies beyond our reach. In the face of challenges, we cultivate resilience, not only for our children but also within ourselves, embodying the stoic virtues of wisdom and courage.

In this way, we transform our approach, turning obstacles into opportunities for growth and understanding. Each moment of difficulty serves as a reminder of the nature of existence: that while we may not master every circumstance, we can master our response to them. We learn to remain steadfast amidst the chaos, drawing upon the inner strength that Stoicism teaches. By cultivating a mindset rooted in acceptance and purposeful action, we create a sanctuary of calm for ourselves and our children, navigating the complexities of life with unwavering resolve.

Recognizing What We Can and Cannot Control in SPD
Recognizing what lies within our grasp and what remains outside our control is a cornerstone of Stoic philosophy, especially for parents navigating the complexities of Sensory Processing Disorder. In the tumult of daily life, the instinctive urge to shield our children from discomfort can easily morph into a relentless pursuit of change. Yet, this pursuit, though steeped in love, often leads to frustration and despair. The sensory experiences that challenge our children are woven into the very fabric of existence. They are not problems to be solved but realities to be acknowledged.

The chaos of sensory overload is a natural occurrence, one that will persist regardless of our well-meaning attempts to alter it. Thus, it becomes paramount to distinguish between what we can influence and what we must accept. Our power lies not in the eradication of sensory triggers but in the cultivation of our responses to them. We can create environments that foster comfort and calm, designing spaces that account for sensory sensitivities. We can establish routines that provide a semblance of order amid the unpredictability of sensory experiences.

Moreover, equipping our children with coping strategies is a vital act of empowerment. By teaching them how to navigate their sensory world, we instill resilience and self-efficacy. This proactive stance is not passive resignation; it is an assertion of our agency in a landscape that often feels overwhelming. We act with intention, focusing our energies on the aspects of our lives we can influence while relinquishing the weight of attempting to control the uncontrollable.

In this journey, clarity of purpose becomes our guiding light. We must define our goals with precision, aligning our actions with our values and principles. Each moment of struggle presents an opportunity for growth—not only for our children but for ourselves as well. The resilience we cultivate in the face of adversity is a testament to our strength, fortifying our commitment to support our children without losing ourselves in the process.

As we embrace this Stoic mindset, we learn to navigate the seas of uncertainty with a steady hand. We find peace in recognizing that while we cannot eliminate chaos, we can find tranquility within it. Letting go of the need to control allows us to focus on nurturing our children and empowering ourselves, forging a path that honors both their journey and our own.

Reframing Expectations for Yourself and Your Child
Reframing ones expectations is a cornerstone of Stoic thought, particularly in the face of challenges like Sensory Processing Disorder (SPD). It is vital for parents to understand that the journey of raising a child with SPD is not a linear path marked by a series of fixes. Instead, it is a complex landscape that demands flexibility, patience, and acceptance of the inherent uncertainties of life.

In the realm of parenting, it is easy to succumb to the illusion that relentless effort can overcome every obstacle. The Stoic perspective urges us to recognize that some conditions, such as SPD, are not problems to be solved but realities to be navigated. This understanding cultivates a sense of realism in our expectations, allowing parents to embrace the notion that while they cannot change certain aspects of their child's sensory experiences, they can influence how these challenges are managed.

Letting go of unrealistic expectations does not signify defeat; rather, it is an act of wisdom and strength. It is the recognition that peace lies not in the relentless pursuit of an unattainable ideal but in accepting and working within the bounds of reality. By adjusting their desires to align with what is possible, parents can reduce the frustration that often accompanies unmet expectations. This shift in mindset allows for a more compassionate and patient approach to parenting, where the focus is on progress rather than perfection.

Stoicism reminds us that every small step forward is a victory worth celebrating. Improvement may come slowly and in unexpected ways, but each advance, no matter how incremental, signifies growth and resilience. It is essential for parents to cultivate an attitude of gratitude for these moments, recognizing them as part of their child's unique journey.

Stoicism teaches us the value of self-reflection and emotional resilience. By engaging in regular introspection, parents can better understand their responses to the challenges they face. This self-awareness can help them maintain composure in difficult moments, fostering a calm environment that is conducive to their child's development.

Ultimately, the Stoic approach provides parents with the tools to cultivate a mindset that prioritizes acceptance, patience, and resilience. By reframing expectations, they can navigate the complexities of SPD with grace, allowing both themselves and their child to thrive amidst the challenges of life.

Emotional Regulation through Stoicism
The Stoic Approach to Emotions

The core tenet of Stoicism lies in the understanding that our emotional experiences stem not from the external events themselves but from the judgments we apply to those events. Frustration, for instance, emerges not from the situation at hand but from our interpretation of it. In moments of strong emotional upheaval, it is essential to recognize that our perceptions shape our experiences. By consciously adjusting our judgments, we can exercise the power to transform our emotional responses.

In the context of parenting a child with Sensory Processing Disorder (SPD), this Stoic insight assumes profound importance. The sensory overload experienced by our child may appear overwhelming, yet it is crucial to acknowledge that this distress is not an unchangeable reality; rather, it is significantly influenced by our own perceptions. By approaching these challenges with the awareness that our emotional responses can be managed, we maintain our composure, resisting the urge to be carried away by waves of frustration.

It is imperative to clarify that the Stoic approach does not endorse the suppression of emotions. Instead, it emphasizes the need to observe our feelings without permitting them to govern our actions or incite hasty reactions. By fostering a mindful awareness of our emotional state, we can better navigate our responses and cultivate a nurturing environment for ourselves and our children. This practice of emotional regulation enhances our resilience, while simultaneously modeling for our children the vital lesson that, although they may not control the external circumstances, they possess the power to shape their responses. In this way, we embody the Stoic principle of maintaining calm in chaos, guiding ourselves and our children toward a more harmonious existence amidst the tumult of life.

Developing Emotional Resilience

Emotional resilience is not merely an abstract concept; it is a discipline that demands our commitment and effort. In the stormy seas of parenting, where sensory overload and challenging behaviors can threaten to capsize our composure, we must cultivate an unwavering inner strength. This strength is forged through the trials we face, much like a blacksmith tempers steel, enhancing its durability through fire and pressure.

As a parent, one must embrace the inevitability of chaos and disarray. Recognizing that adversity is not a hindrance but rather an opportunity for growth allows us to channel our energies toward developing a steady demeanor. Each moment of overwhelm can be seen as a chance to practice restraint and cultivate serenity. By prioritizing our emotional stability, we can create a fortress of calm that not only protects us but also envelops our children in a sense of security.

The teachings of Stoicism remind us that our responses to external turmoil define our emotional landscape. By focusing on what we can control—our thoughts, actions, and reactions—we can navigate through the noise with clarity and purpose. This mindful approach enables us to remain present, engaged, and supportive, even in the most trying circumstances. As we practice this resilience, we not only shield ourselves from the perils of burnout but also model emotional strength for our children, imparting invaluable lessons in self-regulation and composure.

In nurturing our emotional resilience, we lay the groundwork for a nurturing environment that fosters well-being for all family members. The stability we cultivate within ourselves reverberates through our relationships, creating a harmonious atmosphere that encourages connection and belonging. In this way, emotional resilience becomes a vital force, transforming chaos into a foundation for growth and understanding.

Through the lens of Stoicism, we recognize that the challenges we face are not merely obstacles but essential components of our journey. By embracing this perspective, we can find strength in vulnerability and learn to thrive amid uncertainty, ultimately enriching our family dynamic and enhancing the bonds we share.

Teaching Emotional Regulation to Children with SPD
Emotional resilience stands as an essential skill, one that can be cultivated through deliberate and consistent practice over time. For parents, this journey entails the active development of inner strength, enabling them to navigate the tempests of sensory overload and the challenging behaviors that children may exhibit. In the teachings of Stoicism, we recognize that through adversity, we have the opportunity to grow stronger. Just as a muscle must endure resistance to gain strength, so too can our emotional resilience deepen through the trials we face in our parenting.

By nurturing our inner stability, we can maintain a sense of calm amidst chaos. This calmness serves to create a safe harbor for our children, allowing them to feel secure in an unpredictable world. It is through our tranquil presence that we model the fortitude necessary for them to face their own challenges. Each moment of emotional strain is an opportunity for growth, a chance to reinforce our capacity to endure and to support those we love.

Moreover, the practice of emotional resilience is not solely for the benefit of our children; it is vital for our own well-being as parents. By cultivating this resilience, we mitigate the risks of burnout and emotional fatigue, ensuring that we remain fully present and engaged in our children's lives. This presence allows for genuine support, fostering a bond that is essential for healthy development.

In fostering resilience within ourselves, we lay the groundwork for a nurturing and stable environment. Such an environment promotes emotional well-being, not just for the individual, but for the family as a whole. The cultivation of resilience contributes to healthier relationships and a profound sense of belonging, creating a family dynamic that thrives on mutual support and understanding.

Ultimately, the path of emotional resilience is one of commitment and intention. Each challenge faced in the realm of parenting is an invitation to strengthen our resolve, to deepen our capacity for love and understanding. In this way, we not only fortify ourselves but also create a legacy of strength and stability for our children, guiding them toward their own emotional resilience in the face of life's inevitable trials.

Two

Recognizing Sensory Sensitivities in Children

"He who has a why to live can bear almost any how." – **Friedrich Nietzsche**

What is Sensory Processing Disorder?

Defining Sensory Processing Disorder (SPD)
Sensory Processing Disorder (SPD) invites us to reflect deeply on the nature of perception and experience. It is a condition that reveals the intricate workings of the human mind and its connection to the world. At its core, SPD is characterized by the brain's inability to adequately process sensory information, leading to heightened sensitivity to stimuli that most would consider mundane. This disorder is not merely a collection of behavioral quirks; it is a profound challenge that shapes the lived reality of children who face it.

For those children, the world can transform into a cacophony of sensations that overwhelm their senses. The bright lights of a grocery store become blinding; the sounds of chatter, the rustling of bags, the beeping of registers, morph into an unbearable clamor that drowns out their thoughts. Textures that others might find innocuous can feel abrasive against their skin, while smells, rather than being pleasant, can trigger discomfort or even revulsion. In such moments, the world is not merely experienced; it is endured.

In Stoic philosophy, one finds wisdom in the acceptance of one's circumstances. "He who has a why to live can bear almost any how," Nietzsche reminds us. For children grappling with SPD, identifying a purpose or 'why' can be a beacon of strength amid the sensory turmoil. This 'why' may manifest in the form of personal interests, relationships, or the pursuit of understanding their own sensory experiences. It is through this lens of purpose that they can begin to navigate their challenges, transforming overwhelming situations into opportunities for growth and resilience.

Recognizing sensory sensitivities in children is essential, not just for the sake of their comfort, but for fostering a deeper understanding of their unique perspectives. The journey of a child with SPD is not one of mere survival; it is a path of discovery that reveals the profound complexities of human experience. Awareness and support from caregivers, educators, and society at large can create an environment that is not only accommodating but also empowering. In this way, we honor the struggle of those with SPD, recognizing that their journey, while marked by difficulties, is also rich with lessons in patience, empathy, and the human capacity for adaptation.

Moreover, it is essential to cultivate a dialogue around SPD that emphasizes acceptance rather than stigma. By acknowledging the realities of sensory sensitivities, we can foster a culture that prioritizes understanding and compassion. Children with SPD can teach us invaluable lessons about the nature of perception and the importance of creating spaces that are inclusive for all. In embracing their experiences, we not only aid in their journey but also enrich our own understanding of the diverse tapestry of human life.

Ultimately, the recognition of SPD is a call to action for society to reflect on its values and priorities. It challenges us to create environments that are conducive to well-being, where every individual, regardless of their sensory processing abilities, can thrive. In doing so, we honor the essence of what it means to be human—navigating a complex world with grace, courage, and purpose.

Types of Sensory Sensitivities
Recognizing sensory sensitivities in children is a crucial endeavor, particularly for those affected by Sensory Processing Disorder (SPD). Within this realm, two primary types of sensitivities emerge: hypersensitivity and hyposensitivity.

Hypersensitivity is characterized by intense reactions to sensory inputs that others may find manageable. A child exhibiting hypersensitivity may cover their ears in response to what they perceive as an unbearable cacophony, or they may experience distress from the feel of a fabric against their skin, a sensation that others might regard as benign. Such reactions are not mere whims; they stem from an innate response to stimuli that can evoke anxiety and provoke avoidance. In this state, the world can appear as a daunting place, filled with overwhelming sensations that hinder participation in daily activities. The stoic approach teaches us that while these reactions are real and significant, they are also opportunities for growth and understanding. Accepting the child's experiences as valid, caregivers can foster resilience and coping mechanisms, guiding them through their discomfort with patience and wisdom.

Conversely, hyposensitivity presents itself in a different light. Children with this sensitivity may overlook stimuli that others readily acknowledge, or they may actively seek out intense sensory experiences to feel a sense of connection and engagement with their surroundings. A loud noise might go unnoticed, while the child may gravitate towards activities that provide deep pressure or vigorous movement, such as crashing into soft surfaces or spinning in circles. These behaviors are not mere antics; they are a quest for sensory input that helps them achieve a state of balance and grounding. Recognizing this drive is paramount, for it allows caregivers to channel these impulses into constructive activities that not only fulfill the child's sensory needs but also promote their overall well-being.

Understanding these types of sensory sensitivities is not just an academic exercise; it is a pathway to empathy and effective support. By discerning how SPD manifests within a child, caregivers can develop tailored strategies that respect the child's unique sensory experiences. This approach embodies the stoic principle of aligning actions with understanding, allowing for a response that is both compassionate and practical. As caregivers learn to navigate these complexities, they enable children with SPD to thrive in environments that may otherwise feel hostile or overwhelming. In this journey, patience, awareness, and adaptability become essential virtues, guiding both the caregiver and the child towards a more harmonious existence in a sensory-rich world.

The Impact of SPD on Everyday Life

Sensory sensitivities profoundly shape the daily existence of a child, weaving through the fabric of their experiences in ways that can often be overlooked. In social settings, the weight of overwhelming stimuli can bear heavily on a child, rendering interactions fraught with anxiety. The noise of laughter, the brightness of lights, and the unpredictability of movement can transform what might be a joyful gathering into a battleground of discomfort. In such moments, the child may retreat inward, struggling to process the cacophony around them while yearning for connection.

The educational environment presents its own unique challenges, as the multitude of sensory inputs can disrupt a child's ability to focus. The very essence of learning, which is rooted in engagement and exploration, can become stifled by the relentless assault of sensory overload. Sounds that others dismiss as background noise become intrusive, and the vibrant colors of classroom displays may appear overly stimulating, hindering the child's capacity to absorb knowledge. This continual struggle often breeds frustration, not only within the child but also among caregivers who witness their loved one grappling with circumstances that seem manageable to others.

Recognizing these sensitivities is not merely an act of acknowledgment; it is an opportunity for proactive intervention. Parents, equipped with the understanding of their child's unique sensory landscape, can establish structured routines that offer predictability in an unpredictable world. Incorporating sensory breaks into the child's day allows them to recalibrate, to find solace amidst the chaos. Such measures can diminish the likelihood of overwhelming situations, transforming potential stressors into manageable encounters.

In addressing these sensitivities, families cultivate a more harmonious existence. The child is afforded the chance to navigate their environment with greater ease, leading to improved emotional well-being. As frustrations lessen and connections deepen, the bonds within the family can flourish. Ultimately, the recognition and understanding of sensory sensitivities empower both the child and their caregivers, fostering resilience in the face of challenge and promoting a life characterized by greater serenity and mutual support. In this way, the journey through sensory sensitivities becomes not just a struggle, but a pathway to deeper understanding and connection.

The Stoic Perspective on Sensory Sensitivities

Accepting the Reality of Sensory Challenges

Accepting the reality of sensory challenges is a crucial step in the Stoic approach to parenting. Recognizing that sensory processing difficulties are an inherent part of your child's life invites us to confront the truth of their existence. Such challenges are not merely obstacles to overcome but rather aspects of the human experience that require our acknowledgment and understanding.

In the face of these realities, it is vital to distinguish between what we can control and what we cannot. We cannot dictate our child's sensory experiences or eliminate the triggers that cause discomfort. However, we possess the power to shape our reactions, attitudes, and responses. Acceptance does not equate to surrender; it is an active engagement with the present moment. This engagement allows us to channel our energies toward constructive actions rather than futile resistance.

By embracing the notion of sensory sensitivities, we allow ourselves to cultivate patience and empathy. We recognize that these challenges are not personal failings but rather differences in how our children perceive and interact with the world. This understanding fosters a compassionate environment where both parent and child can thrive. It encourages us to seek solutions while maintaining an attitude of equanimity.

As we navigate this journey, we can develop effective coping strategies that resonate with our child's unique needs. This may involve creating calming spaces, establishing routines, or employing mindfulness techniques that help mitigate the impact of sensory overload. Each step taken in acceptance strengthens our resolve and enhances our capacity for resilience.

In the practice of Stoicism, we find solace in the knowledge that our responses define our experience. Acknowledging sensory challenges empowers us to approach them with clarity and purpose. We learn to view them not as burdens but as opportunities for growth—both for our children and for ourselves. By fostering acceptance, we create a nurturing atmosphere that promotes healing and understanding, paving the way for a harmonious coexistence with the realities of sensory sensitivities. Through this lens, we not only support our children's journeys but also embark on our own path of personal growth and emotional fortitude.

Shifting from Frustration to Understanding

I was caught in the grip of frustration for a long time. It came out in short, sudden bursts of exasperation and in the sad, sinking feeling that my son was just not responding to the reasonable requests we were putting before him. I must admit that my transition to our new normal took longer than I would have liked. As a dad, I wanted to be there for him, but I felt woefully unprepared and underqualified in the parenting department.

I sought understanding through social media, joining groups of parents similarly trying to make sense of their children's Sensory Processing Disorders (SPD). However, their experiences often felt different from mine. The advice we received from pediatricians and other doctors was often off-base, and the psychologists' insights also missed the mark. I felt like I was walking down a darkened path, uncertain of my next step.

I submerged myself in SPD literature, dissecting its strategies, savoring its techniques, and tasting its narratives of triumph—hoping that something would resonate with our reality. Yet, none of the fancy fixes seemed to fit my son. I was left feeling formless and unsupported.

Then, one sunny morning, while swinging my son at the park, I heard a whisper of insight. two vital truths all of a sudden made sense. One: I could only control what was mine to control. I could not dictate my son's event-driven emotional responses. But I could work on my own event-driven responses. Two: My son was not "bad" for being out of control. He was controlled by something beyond his control, It wasn't his fault, and no amount of anger or frustration from me would help him., He could no more control how he was reacting to certain events than i could control how he was reacting.

At that moment of clarity, I accepted the truth of what I could not alter—the conditions and my son's behavior in response to them. I then concentrated my efforts on the critically important task of making my own behavior present a more positive role model to him. Up until that point, I had not done a good job of it. My reactions to him had been unhelpfully tinged with frustration, and I had to resolve that first before I could move into the next upcycle part of the model, which is the transition from negativity to a place of understanding. That is where I really try to reach him and where I try to be a better father, a more present emotional protector and confidant.

"True protection is not found in controlling others, but in understanding how our reactions shape their world." - **The Philosophical Dad**

As soon as I removed him from the stimulus that was overwhelming him, he immediately settled. It was like the Pavlov's dog moment in our lives—stimulus leads to a response, but by changing the stimulus, we could change the response. The pattern was clear: I controlled my reaction, and he could finally start to calm down. It wasn't an instant fix, but it was a start—a small but powerful shift in how we both responded to the world around us.

This experience taught me a profound lesson about the power of presence and empathy in parenting. It's easy to get caught up in the chaos of managing SPD, but it's the moments when we stop to recognize what's truly in our control—our own actions—that make the biggest difference.

Recognizing sensory sensitivities in children requires a profound shift in perspective, one that aligns with Stoic principles. Life presents us with challenges, and sensory overload is merely one of its manifestations. Instead of perceiving it as an insurmountable obstacle that disrupts tranquility, we can embrace it as an inherent part of the human experience, an opportunity to cultivate patience and empathy.

The Stoics remind us that our reactions define our experience. It is not the sensory overload itself that disturbs our peace, but rather our interpretation of it. By reframing our understanding of a child's sensory difficulties, we transition from a mindset of frustration to one of compassion. This shift allows us to engage with the situation thoughtfully rather than reactively.

When a child faces a meltdown triggered by sensory overload, a Stoic approach encourages a deliberate pause. We must seek to comprehend the roots of the child's distress, recognizing it as a natural response rather than an act of rebellion. This understanding fosters a calm presence, which is fundamental in such moments. Instead of surrendering to frustration, we can embody a sense of steadiness and compassion, guiding the child through their tumultuous feelings with grace.

In these instances, we are called to create a nurturing environment, one that reassures the child of their safety and acceptance. By acknowledging their sensory sensitivities and approaching their emotional responses with empathy, we enable them to navigate their challenges with resilience. This supportive framework not only aids the child in processing their experiences but also strengthens the bond of trust between parent and child, fostering emotional regulation and stability.

In embracing a Stoic perspective, we equip ourselves to handle the complexities of childhood sensitivities with a calm heart and a clear mind. Through understanding and patience, we can transform moments of distress into opportunities for growth, both for ourselves and for the children we care for.

Building Emotional Resilience

Sensory sensitivities in children present unique challenges that require not only understanding but also a steadfast approach rooted in Stoic principles. The experience of raising a child with Sensory Processing Disorder (SPD) can evoke a range of emotions in caregivers, from frustration to helplessness. Yet, it is in these moments of trial that the Stoic philosophy shines most brightly, offering tools to cultivate emotional resilience.

Patience is a central tenet of Stoicism. It reminds us that the external world is often beyond our control, and the reactions of our children to sensory stimuli are no exception. By embracing this understanding, parents can approach each situation with a sense of calm acceptance rather than resistance. This mindset allows caregivers to remain composed, modeling a steady presence that children can rely on during their moments of distress.

Adaptability, another pillar of Stoicism, encourages parents to remain open to change. Each child's experience with SPD is unique, requiring caregivers to adjust their responses and strategies continually. By remaining flexible and responsive rather than rigid, parents can create an environment that respects and honors their child's sensory needs, fostering a sense of safety and trust.

Mindfulness is a practice that Stoics have long espoused. Taking a moment to pause before reacting can transform the dynamics of challenging interactions. This practice allows parents to reflect on their internal state and choose responses that are constructive and nurturing. Such emotional regulation not only alleviates immediate stress but also demonstrates to children the importance of self-control and thoughtful action in the face of adversity.

The strength of a parent's emotional resilience plays a pivotal role in shaping a child's development. When parents exhibit steadiness, they create a secure environment that enables children to explore their own reactions to sensory stimuli without fear. This sense of safety encourages children to face their challenges with courage, ultimately fostering greater self-confidence as they learn to navigate the complexities of their environment.

As parents embody Stoic virtues, they lay the groundwork for their children to develop essential life skills. The lessons learned through observation—how to remain calm in chaos, how to adapt to changing circumstances, and how to respond thoughtfully—become ingrained in their children's emotional toolkit. This process not only strengthens familial bonds but also equips the next generation to face the unpredictable nature of life with resilience and grace.

In cultivating emotional resilience grounded in Stoicism, parents and children alike embark on a shared journey of growth. Through the practice of patience, adaptability, mindfulness, and emotional steadiness, they forge a path that not only addresses the challenges of sensory sensitivities but also prepares them to embrace the broader complexities of existence. In this way, the enduring teachings of Stoicism resonate, providing a framework for enduring strength amid the trials of life.

The Role of Observation and Empathy in Understanding Sensory Sensitivities

The Power of Observation

To truly grasp the essence of a child's experience with Sensory Processing Disorder, one must embrace the discipline of observation. This practice is not merely a passive activity; it requires an active engagement with the child's world. The observer must cultivate an acute awareness of the child's behaviors, noting the nuances that signal distress or comfort. The environment becomes a canvas on which the child's reactions are painted, revealing a portrait of their sensory sensitivities.

In this process, it is essential to recognize the patterns that emerge from the child's interactions with the world. What stimuli provoke discomfort? What moments bring forth joy or calm? Each observation serves as a clue to unlocking the complexities of the child's perception. This attentive scrutiny is not an act of judgment but rather an exercise in humility and learning. It is through this lens that we begin to understand the emotional landscape that accompanies sensory experiences.

Empathy plays a crucial role alongside observation. It invites us to step into the child's shoes, to experience the world as they do, even if only in our imagination. This effort to connect on a deeper level fosters compassion and patience, guiding us to respond not merely with solutions but with a genuine understanding of the child's plight. The Stoic principle of understanding our shared humanity reminds us that every child's journey is unique, and our role is to support rather than impose.

As we refine our observational skills and deepen our empathetic engagement, we become better equipped to make meaningful adjustments to the child's environment. These adjustments, whether they involve modifying sensory inputs or creating safe spaces for retreat, are not trivial changes; they are gestures of profound care that honor the child's experience. This process is a testament to the Stoic belief in the power of reasoned action — responding to the needs of the child with thoughtful deliberation rather than impulsive reactions.

In fostering this nurturing and adaptive environment, we allow the child to navigate their sensory world with greater ease. The aim is not to eliminate the challenges of sensory sensitivities but to provide the child with tools and support that empower them to thrive. It is through the unwavering commitment to observation and empathy that we can cultivate a space where the child feels seen, understood, and ultimately, more capable of engaging with the world around them. Thus, we embody the Stoic ideal of resilience, transforming challenges into opportunities for growth and connection.

Empathy and Connection

Empathy, in the context of Stoic philosophy, stands as a pillar of human interaction, especially between parent and child. It is an expression of deep understanding, a recognition of shared experience, and a commitment to respond with care and compassion. When a child is overwhelmed by the cacophony of sensory stimuli, their ability to articulate their distress may falter. They may feel trapped within a whirlwind of sensations, unable to find the words that would convey their turmoil. In such moments, the role of a parent shifts from mere observer to a crucial ally.

Rather than succumbing to frustration or impatience, a Stoic parent recognizes this as an opportunity for connection. The child's distress is not a personal affront but a call for understanding. By acknowledging the child's sensory struggles, the parent affirms their feelings, validating an experience that may seem alien to outsiders. This acknowledgment is not merely a gesture; it is a bridge that fosters trust and emotional safety. Through simple acts of kindness—offering a calming presence, creating a quiet space, or employing gentle soothing techniques—the parent becomes a source of comfort.

The Stoic mindset teaches us that while we cannot dictate the feelings or reactions of others, we possess the power to extend our understanding. In the face of a child's sensory overload, we can choose to respond with patience and compassion. This response not only deepens the emotional bond but also serves as a lesson in emotional regulation for the child. They learn that their feelings are worthy of recognition and that they are not alone in their overwhelming experiences.

By practicing empathy, we do more than simply provide immediate relief; we instill resilience. Children who feel supported in their distress are more likely to develop the tools necessary to navigate their emotions in the future. They come to understand that discomfort is a part of life, but so too is the capacity for connection and support. This nurturing environment cultivates emotional intelligence, teaching children the importance of compassion for themselves and others.

In fostering such connections, we prepare our children not only to face their sensory challenges but also to build healthy relationships in their lives. The strength of the parent-child bond, reinforced through understanding and empathy, becomes a foundation upon which they can construct their emotional well-being. These lessons, rooted in the principles of Stoicism, extend far beyond the immediate moment, shaping the character and resilience of the child as they grow into adulthood. Thus, in the practice of empathy, we find a pathway to profound connection and enduring strength that benefits both parent and child alike.

Creating a Sensory-Friendly Environment

Creating a sensory-friendly environment for children with Sensory Processing Disorder (SPD) calls for deliberate action grounded in the understanding that while we cannot control every facet of existence, we can shape our surroundings to foster tranquility. The adjustment of lighting serves as a fundamental step; opting for softer, warmer tones can transform a harsh environment into one that envelops the child in comfort. This change is not merely aesthetic but a profound acknowledgment of the influence that gentle illumination has on the psyche.

Noise, too, demands our attention. The world is filled with cacophony that can overwhelm the senses, igniting anxiety and distress. By consciously managing sound levels, we create an auditory landscape conducive to calm. This is not to suggest that silence is the ultimate goal, but rather a balanced harmony that allows the child to feel secure amidst the natural symphony of life.

The provision of sensory tools is equally vital in this endeavor. Noise-canceling headphones, weighted blankets, and textured items are not mere accessories; they are instruments of stability. In moments of distress, these tools offer a lifeline, providing the child with the means to regain composure and find solace. It is through these thoughtful provisions that we affirm our commitment to their well-being.

Stoicism teaches us that the external environment can be molded to support our inner peace. By taking these proactive measures, we cultivate a sanctuary where the child can explore the world with a sense of safety and assurance. This nurturing environment not only enhances the child's ability to cope with sensory challenges but also strengthens the emotional bonds within the family.

As we create this space, we recognize the profound impact of our actions. The effort to reduce sensory triggers and promote a calming atmosphere is not a trivial pursuit; it is a testament to our understanding of the complexities of existence and our dedication to fostering resilience. In doing so, we not only elevate the child's experience but also enrich the collective harmony of the household, allowing all members to thrive.

Helen Keller

Helen Keller's life is a powerful testament to the resilience of the human spirit and the extraordinary capacity for growth, even in the face of profound sensory challenges. Born deaf and blind, Keller was thrust into a world that, for most, is difficult to imagine—where sounds are unheard, sights are unseen, and communication feels like an insurmountable wall. Yet, with the relentless dedication of her teacher, Anne Sullivan, Keller not only learned to navigate this world but to engage with it in ways that seemed impossible. Her journey wasn't simply about overcoming obstacles—it was about connecting, understanding, and being understood. The drive to forge those connections was both simple and profound, and it was this purpose that fueled her every step.

The story of Keller's determination is a reminder of the power of purpose in overcoming adversity. Just as she faced unimaginable sensory barriers, those of us navigating the complexities of sensory processing challenges know how easy it is to feel isolated, confused, and misunderstood. The daily barrage of distorted sounds, blinding lights, and overwhelming textures can leave anyone feeling lost in a world that doesn't seem to accommodate their needs. But Keller's life proves that resilience, when paired with a sense of purpose, can transform even the most daunting struggles into powerful tools for change. In time, she not only became a renowned writer and activist but also a fierce advocate for the rights of those with disabilities—proving that perseverance, combined with unwavering belief in one's own worth, can overcome even the greatest challenges.

Keller once said, *"It is a terrible thing to see and have no vision."* This sentiment cuts to the core of the experience for many individuals with sensory processing disorder (SPD). Just as Keller's world was shaped by the lack of sight and sound, those with SPD often face a reality where sensory input is distorted or overwhelming. In both cases, the struggle is not simply one of communication, but of finding a way to exist in a world that seems out of reach. But Keller's story reminds us that the key to overcoming this dissonance lies in connection—in reaching out for support, in finding those who understand, and in fostering a sense of belonging.

Keller's relationship with Anne Sullivan serves as a powerful example of what it means to support someone through their sensory journey. Sullivan didn't simply teach Keller to communicate—she provided a bridge between Keller's isolated world and the external one. Her methods were creative, innovative, and deeply personal. For those of us supporting loved ones with SPD, this relationship highlights the importance of patience, empathy, and understanding. It underscores the profound impact that a dedicated, compassionate caregiver can have in helping someone find their voice, navigate sensory challenges, and unlock their potential. The presence of such support systems—whether in the form of family, teachers, or peers—can make all the difference in fostering resilience and independence.

But Keller's story goes beyond personal triumph—it is a call for societal change. Keller fought not only for her own rights but for the rights of all individuals with disabilities. She recognized that society's narrow approach to communication and interaction often leaves out those with unique sensory needs. Just as Keller advocated for the inclusion and recognition of people with disabilities, we too must strive for a world that acknowledges and adapts to the diverse sensory experiences of individuals with SPD. By embracing inclusivity and empathy, we can create environments where everyone—no matter their sensory experience—feels valued and empowered.

Ultimately, Keller's life is not just a story of personal triumph; it is a call to action. It teaches us that resilience is not only about enduring difficulties but also about the connections we make along the way. By fostering a deeper understanding of sensory challenges, encouraging empathy, and building support networks, we can help those with SPD navigate their unique experiences. And perhaps, like Keller, they will find their own voice in a world that may sometimes feel deafening, but that, with the right support, can be made more inclusive and understanding for everyone

Three

The Power of Patience

"Patience is not simply the ability to wait – it's how we behave while we're waiting." – **Joyce Meyer**

The Importance of Patience in Parenting

Patience as a Stoic Virtue

In the realm of Stoic philosophy, patience emerges not as a mere waiting game but as an essential practice that embodies strength and discipline. It is a conscious act that requires the cultivation of inner calm and rational thought in the face of life's inevitable trials. The Stoics teach that our disturbances arise not from external events but from the judgments we impose upon them. For parents navigating the complexities of raising a child with Sensory Processing Disorder (SPD), this understanding becomes profoundly significant.

When confronted with the overwhelming sensations that can engulf a child with SPD, parents stand at a crossroads where the choice of response is crucial. To react in haste, fueled by frustration or impatience, is to fall into a common pitfall. Yet, to respond with a measured approach—infused with patience, understanding, and emotional steadiness—demonstrates a commitment to embodying Stoic virtues. This conscious decision not only influences the parent's well-being but also serves as a powerful model for the child, illustrating how to navigate life's challenges with resilience.

In this context, patience becomes synonymous with acceptance. It invites parents to embrace the reality that progress may not follow a linear path. Instead of perceiving time as a relentless race toward an endpoint, Stoicism encourages us to perceive each moment as an opportunity for growth and learning. The trials faced in parenting are not merely obstacles but are pivotal moments that enrich the parent-child relationship, fostering deeper understanding and connection.

In raising a child with SPD, the cultivation of patience allows parents to sidestep the urge for immediate solutions. It nurtures an environment where thoughtful engagement with each sensory challenge can occur. Parents learn that it is not the speed of progress that matters, but the quality of their responses and the integrity of their actions. This steadfast approach not only supports the child's development but also reinforces the parent's resolve, creating a shared journey of growth.

In embracing patience, both parent and child can thrive together, learning to appreciate the unfolding process of life rather than fixating solely on the outcomes. This shared experience, grounded in Stoic principles, fosters resilience, allowing them to face future challenges with a calm and deliberate approach, embodying the true essence of patience.

Patience with Yourself

Patience with oneself emerges as a profound necessity in the intricate landscape of parenting, particularly when navigating the complexities of a child with Sensory Processing Disorder (SPD). The journey is fraught with challenges that can easily lead to self-reproach and frustration. In this context, Stoicism offers a philosophical framework that encourages individuals to cultivate self-compassion and patience. It invites us to reflect on the nature of our existence and our responses to life's vicissitudes.

The Stoic principle of accepting the things we cannot control resonates deeply with parents who grapple with feelings of inadequacy. It is a reminder that external circumstances, including the unique needs of a child with SPD, are often beyond our influence. Thus, the weight of responsibility can feel overwhelming, particularly when it manifests in a child's social interactions or academic challenges. Yet, in embracing Stoicism, one learns to delineate between what is within our power and what lies beyond it. This understanding fosters a sense of liberation, allowing parents to release the debilitating grip of guilt and blame.

Moreover, the Stoics taught that personal growth is a continual process, achieved through practice and reflection. This notion is particularly relevant for parents, who must navigate their own emotional landscapes while supporting their child. Just as one would patiently guide a child in developing coping strategies for sensory overload, so too must one extend that same grace to oneself. Acknowledging personal limitations and imperfections does not equate to failure; rather, it signifies a commitment to growth and resilience.

In this journey, patience transforms from a simple virtue into an essential practice. It becomes a way of honoring both the struggles we face and the efforts we make. By recognizing and celebrating small victories, parents can cultivate a sense of progress that nurtures self-acceptance. This recognition allows for a more profound understanding of the shared human experience of struggle, fostering empathy and connection not only with oneself but also with others who traverse similar paths.

In essence, patience with oneself is not an endpoint but a vital aspect of the ongoing journey of parenting. It embodies the Stoic belief that life will present us with trials, yet through perseverance and self-compassion, we can rise to meet them. By adopting this mindset, parents can transform their relationship with themselves, viewing each moment of difficulty as an opportunity for growth and insight, ultimately enriching their journey alongside their child.

The Long-Term Rewards of Patience

In the tapestry of life, patience weaves a thread that is often overlooked in the rush of modern existence. The immediate discomfort that accompanies the practice of patience can feel like an insurmountable weight, especially when faced with the unpredictable nature of sensory challenges that disrupt the harmony of daily life. Yet, in this very struggle lies a profound truth: the cultivation of resilience is not an instantaneous phenomenon but rather a gradual blossoming that unfolds over time.

The Stoics imparted wisdom that resonates through the ages, encouraging us to perceive challenges as opportunities for growth. This perspective invites us to embrace the discomfort of the present moment, recognizing that each trial is a stepping stone toward greater fortitude. In nurturing patience within children, we are not merely asking them to endure; we are guiding them to construct a framework of coping mechanisms and emotional regulation skills. These skills, forged in the crucible of experience, become essential tools that will accompany them into adulthood, enabling them to navigate the complexities of life with grace and assurance.

As time progresses, the fruits of patience begin to manifest in subtle yet profound ways. Parents may find solace in observing their child's evolving ability to confront sensory challenges with increasing confidence. This transformation is not merely a reflection of the child's growth but also a testament to the dedication and steadfastness of the parent. The journey becomes a shared odyssey, where both child and parent cultivate a deeper understanding of themselves and their relationship with the world.

The essence of patience lies in its capacity to foster a sense of inner peace. It invites parents to adopt a long-term perspective, one that transcends the fleeting nature of immediate gratification. In this contemplative space, the act of witnessing a child's growth becomes a source of joy rather than frustration. When parents resist the temptation to rush their child's development, they create an environment where exploration and learning can flourish organically.

This long view fosters optimism, allowing parents to recognize that the seeds sown today will yield a harvest of resilience tomorrow. Each moment of patience is an investment in the future, contributing to a landscape where the child can thrive. In this unfolding narrative, both parent and child are participants in a profound journey of discovery, where patience becomes not just a virtue but a cornerstone of character.

Thus, the long-term rewards of patience illuminate a path toward emotional maturity and stability. They remind us that while the journey may be fraught with challenges, the cultivation of patience ultimately enriches our lives, transforming trials into triumphs and fostering a legacy of resilience that echoes through generations. In the grand tapestry of existence, patience emerges as a guiding light, illuminating the way toward a more harmonious and fulfilling life.

Thomas Edison – Perseverance Through Patience and Setbacks

Thomas Edison's life is a testament to the power of perseverance through patience and setbacks. His relentless pursuit to create the lightbulb is one of the most compelling narratives in the history of innovation. Far from being deterred by the myriad of failures he encountered, Edison viewed each setback as an integral part of the journey toward success. He famously stated, "I have not failed. I've just found 10,000 ways that won't work." This perspective is not just about optimism; it embodies the essence of resilience, a quality crucial for overcoming challenges.

For parents of children with Sensory Processing Disorder (SPD), Edison's story serves as a powerful reminder of the importance of patience and persistence. The journey may often feel daunting, with progress appearing slow and setbacks a constant reality. However, just as Edison recognized that every failure brought him closer to his goal, parents can view the hurdles they face as opportunities for growth. Embracing the challenges associated with raising a child with SPD can foster resilience, both in themselves and in their children.

Edison's mindset reflects a broader Stoic philosophy, which teaches that challenges are not obstacles but stepping stones to personal development. By adopting this outlook, parents can instill the same resilience in their children. Each struggle with sensory experiences can be reframed as a chance for learning and adaptation. The road to progress may be winding and fraught with difficulties, but it is precisely through these trials that strength and character are forged.

In the face of adversity, patience becomes an invaluable asset. Edison's unwavering belief in the power of persistence not only led to monumental inventions but also to a profound understanding of the human spirit's capacity to endure and thrive. For parents navigating the complexities of SPD, holding onto that belief can transform the journey from one of frustration to one of hope and growth. Just as Edison's perseverance illuminated the world, so too can your unwavering support and patience illuminate the path for your child, leading to their eventual success and fulfillment.

Building Long-Term Resilience in Children

"Patience is not the ability to wait, but how you act while you're waiting." – Joyce Meyer

The Role of Consistent Patience in Building Resilience

During my travels as a father of a child with Sensory Processing Disorder (SPD) over the last six years, life has obviously been fraught with stress and anxiety. And if you're reading this book, I assume you know exactly how that feels. The Stoic virtue of temperance has been my guiding light through it all. Without patience, nothing will go right. When everything is already hard, when things don't go the direction you hope they will, the ability to simply breathe for a moment, to center yourself, is vital. Remember: God never gives you more than you can handle. And on the other side of what's happening, there's hopefully a stronger, more resilient version of you—or at the very least, a more reflective one. Because when things don't go the way you were hoping, and now it's over, and you have five minutes to sit, you can think back to what happened, how your child reacted, and how you responded to that reaction.

I don't have little personal anecdotes for this chapter, because we all live such different lives. But what I do want to discuss is the story of Sisyphus, a tale that has always struck a chord with me, especially in the context of raising a child with SPD.

In Greek mythology, Sisyphus is condemned to roll a boulder up a hill, only for it to roll back down every time he nears the top. This task is endless and feels completely futile. However, as time passes, Sisyphus learns to accept his punishment with patience, making peace with the process itself. Though the end goal is never reached, it's the act of persevering and continuing to roll the boulder that gives him meaning.

Much like Sisyphus, as parents, we often feel like we're pushing a boulder uphill. Every time we feel like we're getting somewhere with our child's sensory processing or emotional regulation, it feels like something knocks the boulder back down the hill. The frustration, the repetition, the constant starting over—it can be overwhelming. But Sisyphus's story teaches us that sometimes, the task itself is the teacher. It's not about reaching the top of the hill immediately; it's about persevering in the face of adversity, learning patience in the journey, and finding strength in our consistent efforts.

Just like Sisyphus, we may find meaning in the daily effort and the patience that each day requires. Parenting a child with SPD is not about reaching a definitive "end goal" quickly—it's about showing up every day, doing the work, and finding growth in the process. Our efforts to guide, support, and love our children are the true measure of our strength, just as Sisyphus's endless effort ultimately shaped him.

In this journey, we too must find peace in the process. While there may be no clear end in sight, the patience we practice today will build the resilience we need for tomorrow. And like Sisyphus, each time the boulder rolls back down, we have the chance to push it up again, learning something new about ourselves, our child, and the journey we're on together.

> *"The journey is not measured by how close we get to the top, but by how many times we rise to push the boulder up the hill."* – **The Philosophical Dad**

Resilience is not an instantaneous attribute; rather, it is a gradual construction, forged through the crucible of experience and the steady hands of those who guide us. For a child grappling with Sensory Processing Disorder (SPD), resilience emerges not from mere instruction or sporadic intervention but through the accumulation of experiences that teach them how to navigate a world filled with sensory challenges. Each encounter with difficulty serves as a building block, and the role of consistent patience in this process cannot be underestimated.

When parents approach these challenges with unwavering patience, they cultivate an environment in which the child perceives obstacles not as threats, but as opportunities for growth. This patient response serves as a powerful reminder that challenges are part of the human experience, and through thoughtful engagement, they can be overcome. Each instance where a child is supported through their sensory struggles reinforces their belief in their own capabilities, helping them to develop coping mechanisms that will serve them well throughout life.

The essence of this practice lies in its consistency. For children with SPD, sensory sensitivities can provoke a wide spectrum of emotional reactions. It is within the framework of a predictable and supportive environment that they can begin to construct their resilience. As they learn that their reactions, no matter how overwhelming, are met with understanding and calmness, they develop a profound sense of trust in their caregivers. This trust is the bedrock upon which resilience is built.

In time, this steady approach nurtures emotional fortitude. It teaches children that while they may encounter difficulties, they are not alone. The steadfast patience of their parents serves as an anchor in turbulent times, allowing the child to explore their environment with a sense of security. Thus, the practice of consistent patience transforms each sensory challenge into a lesson in strength, reinforcing the notion that they can emerge from adversity stronger and more capable.

In the grand tapestry of life, resilience is woven through repeated threads of experience, patience, and support. Each moment of calmness in the face of sensory upheaval contributes to a child's ability to confront future challenges with greater confidence. As they learn to rely on the steady presence of their caregivers, they cultivate not just resilience but a deeper understanding of the human capacity to adapt and grow in the face of adversity. In this way, consistent patience is not merely a response; it is a profound investment in the development of a resilient spirit.

Teaching Your Child to See Challenges as Opportunities for Growth

Teaching your child to perceive challenges as opportunities for growth is indeed one of the most profound gifts a parent can impart. This approach resonates with the principles of Stoic philosophy, which posits that adversity is not merely an obstacle but a catalyst for personal development. In this context, children who experience Sensory Processing Disorder (SPD) often encounter unique challenges that set them apart from their peers. Instead of allowing these differences to foster feelings of inadequacy or shame, parents can guide their children to embrace these moments as valuable lessons in self-discovery.

When a child faces sensory overload in a bustling environment, the instinct may be to view the experience as a setback. However, the Stoic perspective encourages reframing such situations. Parents can assist their children in recognizing that these challenges are opportunities to cultivate essential skills, such as self-regulation and emotional resilience. For instance, when a child struggles with overwhelming stimuli, they can be taught to utilize techniques like deep breathing or to rely on tools like noise-canceling headphones as methods of self-soothing. This reframing transforms a potentially distressing moment into a practical exercise in coping strategies.

By consistently reinforcing this mindset, parents instill a sense of resilience within their children. They learn that their challenges do not define them but rather contribute to their personal growth. This awareness fosters confidence, equipping them to face sensory difficulties with a sense of agency rather than fear. In nurturing this perspective, parents help their children understand that every obstacle carries the potential for improvement, aligning their experiences with the Stoic ideal that it is not the events themselves that disturb us, but our perceptions of those events. Thus, challenges become stepping stones on the path to greater self-mastery and understanding.

Building a Safe Space for Emotional Expression
Resilience is not just about handling external challenges—it's also about being able to express and process emotions effectively. For children with SPD, emotional expression can often be difficult. When overwhelmed by sensory input, children may struggle to verbalize their feelings or communicate what they need. One of the best ways to build resilience in these children is to create a safe space where they can express their emotions without fear of judgment or frustration.

Patience plays a crucial role here. By patiently allowing children the time they need to express themselves, whether through words, actions, or even physical cues, parents validate their feelings and provide them with the emotional support they need. This emotional security is the foundation upon which resilience is built. When children feel safe expressing their emotions, they develop the skills to process and manage them in the future, making them more resilient in the face of adversity.

Developing Patience Through Practice

Stoic Exercises for Cultivating Patience

Stoicism provides a framework through which individuals can cultivate patience, a virtue essential for navigating the complexities of life, particularly in the context of parenting. Daily reflection serves as a cornerstone of this practice. In the quiet moments of the evening, when the day's events have unfolded, parents should engage in a deliberate examination of their actions and reactions. They must ask themselves: What aspects of the day were within my control? What elements were beyond my influence? This separation fosters a profound understanding that frustration often arises from our fixation on the uncontrollable. By recognizing that our responses are the only domain we truly govern, parents can cultivate a sense of calm, allowing them to approach challenges with a steady mind.

Another vital practice in the Stoic tradition is visualization. This technique involves deliberately imagining potential challenges that may arise in the parenting journey, envisioning how one would ideally respond with patience and composure. By mentally rehearsing these scenarios, parents prepare themselves for the inevitable tests of their patience. Each visualization serves not merely as a mental exercise but as a preparation for reality, reinforcing the resolve to maintain equanimity in the face of adversity. Through this process, parents can gradually transform their instinctual reactions, nurturing a deeper capacity for patience.

These Stoic exercises, rooted in reflection and visualization, empower parents to cultivate patience as a deliberate practice. In doing so, they embody the Stoic principle that while we may not control external events, we possess the power to govern our internal responses. As patience grows through these practices, so too does the ability to navigate the challenges of parenting with grace and resilience.

The Power of Perspective

In the realm of Stoicism, the ability to reframe challenges is not merely a tool but a profound practice that shapes our understanding of the world. When faced with the sensory sensitivities of a child, which may provoke frustration or distress, it is essential for parents to remember that their responses define the experience. Rather than perceiving such moments as personal failings or burdens to be alleviated, parents can choose to recognize these instances as opportunities for growth.

Each episode of difficulty can be seen not as a setback, but as a chance to cultivate patience and resilience. This shift in perspective is not a trivial adjustment; it is a fundamental transformation in how one engages with life's inevitable challenges. For instance, when a child experiences a meltdown in a public setting, parents can reframe this as a poignant reminder of the necessity and value of patience. Such a perspective allows them to detach from the emotional turbulence that the moment invites, enabling a calm and measured response.

By embracing this Stoic principle, parents diminish the emotional burden of the situation, allowing for a more constructive approach. They can guide themselves and their children through the storm of emotions with a steady hand, fostering an environment where resilience is nurtured. Over time, this deliberate practice not only fortifies the parent's own character but also instills a lasting sense of resilience in the child.

Thus, the power of perspective lies in its ability to transform challenges into opportunities for inner strength and growth. In the face of adversity, we are reminded that our reactions wield significant influence over our experiences. By consciously choosing how to perceive each situation, we affirm our capacity for patience, understanding, and ultimately, tranquility.

Using Patience to Build Stronger Parent-Child Bonds
Patience is a virtue that serves as a cornerstone in the relationship between parent and child. In the realm of parenting, it is essential to recognize that the manner in which one responds to a child's needs and emotions shapes the very fabric of their bond. When parents embody patience, they exhibit a steadfast commitment to understanding their child's perspective, fostering an environment where the child feels valued and heard. This nurturing approach cultivates a deep sense of safety and security, allowing the child to trust that their feelings will be acknowledged and respected.

In the face of challenges, particularly for children with sensory processing difficulties, this bond becomes even more critical. The child learns through experience that their parent is a source of comfort and guidance. Such assurance empowers them to confront their sensory challenges with greater resilience, knowing that they are not alone in their struggles. The consistent practice of patience not only models resilience but also reinforces the significance of emotional stability within the relationship.

As parents navigate the complexities of raising a child, they must remember that each moment of patience is an investment in their child's emotional foundation. This enduring commitment to understanding and empathy lays the groundwork for a supportive environment, allowing the child to thrive. The strength of the parent-child bond, rooted in trust and patience, becomes a vital support system that endures through the trials of life, equipping the child with the emotional fortitude necessary for growth and development. In the grand tapestry of life, the quiet power of patience weaves a narrative of connection that transcends the challenges faced, fostering a legacy of understanding and love.

Four

Emotional Mastery

"He who is brave is free." – **Seneca**

The Role of Emotional Control in Parenting

Understanding the Stoic Approach to Emotions
Emotional control in parenting, particularly when raising a child with sensory processing disorder, requires a steadfast commitment to the principles of Stoicism. This philosophical approach teaches us that emotions themselves are not the enemy; they are simply responses to our perceptions of events. In the practice of parenting, especially under the strain of sensory overload, it is essential to recognize that our reactions are within our control.

When a child is overwhelmed by stimuli, it is natural for a parent to feel an array of emotions, such as frustration, anxiety, or helplessness. However, Stoic wisdom encourages us to observe these feelings without judgment. By acknowledging our emotional state without letting it govern our behavior, we cultivate a sense of calm and clarity. This composed demeanor becomes a powerful tool, not only for our own well-being but also as a model for our children. In the face of sensory challenges, maintaining a level head not only alleviates our own distress but also instills a sense of security and stability in our children.

The Stoic perspective emphasizes the importance of reframing our judgments. When a child reacts to a loud noise, a parent might initially view this as a failure of their ability to manage the situation. Yet, through the lens of Stoicism, we can shift our perception. Instead of seeing this reaction as a personal setback, we can understand it as an opportunity for growth—both for ourselves and our child. By approaching the moment with patience and empathy, we can help our child navigate their emotions while simultaneously reinforcing our own capacity for resilience.

Moreover, embracing emotional control allows us to respond thoughtfully rather than react impulsively. We can ask ourselves what is truly within our power: our thoughts and responses. The external chaos may be beyond our control, but our inner state remains a domain where we can exercise influence. By practicing this control, we align ourselves with the Stoic ideal of virtue, which is rooted in wisdom, courage, and temperance.

Ultimately, the journey of parenting is laden with challenges, particularly when navigating the complexities of sensory processing disorder. However, by adhering to a Stoic approach to emotions, we not only enhance our own emotional regulation but also empower our children to cultivate their own. In teaching them to respond to their experiences with composure and reflection, we equip them with skills that will serve them throughout their lives. In this way, emotional control becomes not just a personal endeavor but a shared legacy of strength and understanding.

Emotional Control as a Parenting Tool

Emotional control stands as a vital pillar in the practice of effective parenting, transcending mere self-regulation to become a powerful instrument for nurturing a child's growth. In moments of sensory overload, children, particularly those with Sensory Processing Disorder, instinctively seek guidance from their parents. Their reactions become a mirror reflecting the emotional climate set by caregivers. If a parent succumbs to frustration or panic, it can exacerbate the child's distress, leading to further anxiety. Conversely, when a parent embodies calm and composure, they create an oasis of safety, providing the child with a sense of security amidst chaos.

Children are keen observers, absorbing the emotional responses displayed by their caregivers. By demonstrating emotional control, parents impart a crucial lesson: that even in the face of overwhelming circumstances, it is possible to remain grounded. This ability to maintain equanimity not only fosters the child's sense of safety but also equips them with the understanding that emotions can be managed rather than allowed to dictate actions. It teaches resilience, illustrating that the storms of emotion can be weathered with grace.

In addition to fostering a sense of security, emotional control enables parents to approach challenging situations with clarity and purpose. During a child's meltdown triggered by sensory input, a composed parent stands as a beacon of stability. This steadiness allows for a thoughtful evaluation of the situation, facilitating responses that are measured and compassionate rather than impulsive and reactive. Such responses might include creating a quiet retreat, employing calming techniques, or offering soothing words—all grounded in the understanding that the child requires guidance to navigate their emotional landscape.

Furthermore, by embodying emotional control, parents not only manage their own stress but also model essential skills for their children. They demonstrate that emotional regulation is a learned behavior, one that can be cultivated through practice and intention. This modeling is particularly significant for children grappling with sensory challenges, as it equips them with the tools necessary for self-regulation and emotional intelligence.

In essence, emotional control serves as both a personal practice and a parenting strategy that nurtures stability, resilience, and emotional growth. It invites parents to cultivate an environment where children can learn to navigate their feelings, fostering a profound sense of trust and connection that will serve them throughout their lives.

Practical Strategies for Emotional Control
Developing emotional control is a discipline that demands consistent practice and the application of Stoic principles. To cultivate this skill, one can adopt various practical strategies that ground responses in reason rather than impulse.

Mindfulness serves as a cornerstone of emotional regulation. By deliberately taking a moment to pause and breathe deeply, individuals can create a space between stimulus and reaction. This conscious interruption allows for reflection and the opportunity to choose a measured, thoughtful response. In the heat of a stressful moment, especially as a parent, this brief pause can transform an automatic reaction into a deliberate action, fostering an atmosphere of calm amidst chaos.

Another powerful Stoic technique is negative visualization. This method involves mentally rehearsing adverse scenarios, effectively preparing the mind for potential challenges. For parents, envisioning situations that may provoke sensory overload can be particularly beneficial. By anticipating these challenges and mentally rehearsing responses, one can cultivate emotional resilience. This preparation fosters a sense of calm and clarity, enabling parents to navigate stressful moments with patience, rather than succumbing to anxiety.

Journaling is an invaluable practice for enhancing self-awareness and reflection on emotional responses. By documenting thoughts and feelings, parents can identify recurring patterns in their emotional reactions, gaining insight into triggers and areas for improvement. This process not only aids in emotional regulation but also reinforces the Stoic practice of self-examination. Over time, through deliberate reflection and analysis, parents can develop a deeper understanding of themselves, leading to improved emotional control and a more balanced approach to life's inevitable challenges.

Ultimately, the pursuit of emotional control is a journey of self-mastery. Through mindfulness, negative visualization, and journaling, individuals can cultivate a stoic disposition that allows them to face life's trials with equanimity and grace.

Nelson Mandela – The Power of Emotional Mastery in the Face of Adversity

Nelson Mandela's life stands as a powerful example of emotional mastery in the face of profound adversity. After spending 27 years in prison, enduring unimaginable hardships, he emerged not with bitterness or anger, but as a symbol of peace, reconciliation, and the transformative power of emotional resilience. Despite the oppressive environment, the physical pain, and the deep personal sacrifices, Mandela found ways to remain focused on his higher purpose: ending apartheid and fostering unity in South Africa. His ability to regulate his emotions, to not let the external world dictate his inner state, showcases a level of emotional control that is nothing short of extraordinary. In doing so, he exemplified the Stoic principle of maintaining inner peace despite overwhelming external turmoil.

Mandela's story resonates deeply with those of us navigating the challenges of raising a child with Sensory Processing Disorder (SPD). Like Mandela, parents face moments of deep frustration, stress, and overwhelm, often dealing with the emotional turbulence that comes with supporting a child who struggles to process sensory input. Whether it's a meltdown triggered by an unexpected sound or an inability to engage with social situations due to sensory overload, parents, like Mandela, must find a way to maintain emotional resilience. It's easy to get lost in the moment of distress, to feel helpless when our children are struggling, but the key lies in emotional mastery—the ability to stay calm and centered in the face of challenges.

This is not about suppressing emotions or pretending everything is fine. Instead, it's about recognizing the emotions we feel and choosing how to respond to them, with patience and understanding. Just as Mandela faced his struggles with an unwavering commitment to his purpose, parents can navigate the challenges of SPD with a clear sense of purpose: helping their child manage sensory experiences and develop the emotional intelligence necessary to thrive in a world that often feels overwhelming.

"I am not a saint, unless you think of a saint as a sinner who keeps on trying." – **Nelson Mandela**

Mandela's perspective that resilience comes not from perfection but from the continuous effort to persevere, no matter the obstacles. It's a reminder that emotional mastery is not a one-time achievement but a lifelong practice. Just as Mandela kept striving to fulfill his purpose, parents of children with SPD must keep trying—patience, understanding, and emotional resilience are built through repeated effort, even in the face of adversity.

Mandela's legacy teaches us that no matter the external circumstances, we always have control over how we respond. Through the same emotional resilience that carried him through his trials, parents can find the strength to stay present for their children, guiding them with compassion, calmness, and unwavering support. The challenges of SPD are real, but they don't define the journey. It is through emotional mastery that we can create a space for growth and connection, just as Mandela created a path for healing and unity in a divided nation.

Teaching Emotional Regulation to Children with SPD

The Importance of Emotional Awareness

The path to emotional regulation begins with the vital foundation of emotional awareness. It is essential to recognize that before one can master the art of regulating emotions, there must first be a clear understanding of what those emotions entail. For children grappling with sensory processing difficulties, this understanding can be particularly challenging. Their internal experiences may be clouded by a barrage of sensory input, leaving them struggling to articulate feelings or even recognize the moments when they are overwhelmed.

In this endeavor, parents serve as steadfast guides. Their keen observation of a child's behavior is paramount. They must learn to discern the subtle signs of distress that may manifest in fidgeting, awkward body posture, or fleeting expressions of frustration. These indicators are not merely random behaviors; they are critical signals from the child's inner world, deserving of attention and understanding.

Once these cues are identified, the introduction of emotional vocabulary becomes paramount. Providing children with words such as "angry," "frustrated," or "overwhelmed" transforms nebulous feelings into tangible concepts. This linguistic framework does more than merely label emotions; it empowers children, allowing them to articulate their experiences with clarity. In doing so, they begin to navigate their emotional landscapes more effectively, fostering a greater sense of agency in their lives.

As parents engage in this process, they not only enhance their child's ability to express emotions but also deepen their own understanding of their child's needs. This mutual growth nurtures a connection rooted in empathy and awareness, reinforcing the notion that emotional regulation is not a solitary journey. It is a shared endeavor where understanding and communication pave the way for resilience and emotional strength. In this pursuit, the cultivation of emotional awareness stands as a cornerstone, guiding children toward a future where they can meet life's challenges with equanimity and composure.

Normalizing emotions is another essential aspect of fostering emotional awareness.

Normalizing emotions serves as a vital foundation for developing emotional awareness. Children facing sensory processing challenges often grapple with feelings of shame or confusion in response to their heightened emotional states. This burden may lead them to believe that their reactions are unwelcome or abnormal. It is imperative for parents to instill the understanding that emotions are a natural and fundamental aspect of the human condition.

By fostering an environment where emotions are acknowledged rather than feared, parents encourage children to embrace their feelings without judgment. This approach cultivates a sense of safety, enabling children to explore and articulate their emotional experiences openly. Recognizing that emotions, like all things, are transient responses to the stimuli around them empowers children to see themselves as separate from their feelings.

In this light, emotions can be viewed as temporary visitors rather than permanent fixtures. Children learn that while they may experience intense emotional reactions, these feelings do not define their identity. Instead, they can cultivate the skills necessary to navigate their emotional landscape with grace and resilience. This practice of managing emotional responses fosters a profound sense of emotional fortitude, allowing children to approach challenges with a balanced mindset and a deeper understanding of their own humanity. In the end, the cultivation of emotional awareness lays the groundwork for a life marked by equanimity and strength in the face of adversity.

"Emotions are the slaves to the actions of the intellect." - **Epictetus**

Using Stoic Principles to Teach Emotional Regulation
The Stoic practice emphasizes the distinction between what is within our control and what is not. This principle serves as a foundation for teaching emotional regulation, especially for children facing Sensory Processing Disorder (SPD). Children must learn that while external sensory stimuli may be beyond their control, their reactions and thoughts remain firmly within their grasp. This understanding is vital, as it empowers them to navigate their experiences with a sense of agency.

Parents can introduce techniques rooted in Stoic thought to aid children in managing overwhelming sensations. For instance, the practice of deep breathing acts as a bridge to a calmer state of mind. When a child feels overwhelmed, pausing to take measured breaths allows them to create a space between stimulus and reaction, fostering a sense of control. Similarly, counting to ten can serve as a simple yet effective tool, encouraging mindfulness and reflection before responding to the immediate challenge.

For younger children, visual aids and sensory-friendly environments can enhance understanding and practice of emotional regulation. A dedicated "calm-down" corner, equipped with fidget toys or soothing music, provides a tangible space where children can retreat to regain composure. This physical manifestation of Stoic principles reinforces the idea that one can create an internal calm amidst external chaos.

Furthermore, the role of parents as models cannot be overstated. Children are keen observers, often mirroring the behaviors of their caregivers. When a parent demonstrates emotional regulation—maintaining composure during a sensory challenge—they offer a powerful lesson in resilience. This modeling instills the belief that emotional control is attainable, allowing children to internalize these Stoic practices over time.

As children gradually adopt these techniques, they begin to cultivate a mindset that frames their emotional responses as manageable rather than overwhelming. This Stoic approach not only fosters resilience but also nurtures emotional intelligence, equipping children with the tools necessary to navigate a world filled with sensory challenges. Through consistent practice and modeling, the principles of Stoicism can guide children toward a more balanced emotional existence, enabling them to thrive despite external circumstances.

Creating a Routine of Emotional Check-ins

Creating a routine of emotional check-ins is a practice rooted in the understanding that emotions are an integral part of the human experience. For children with Sensory Processing Disorder (SPD), establishing a daily time to reflect on feelings serves not only as a means of communication but also as a pathway to emotional resilience. In this sacred space of dialogue, parents can pose open-ended questions, inviting their children to explore their inner worlds. Inquiry such as "How did you feel today?" or "What made you happy or upset?" encourages the young mind to articulate its complexities.

This practice fosters emotional literacy, allowing children to identify and name their feelings. The act of expressing emotions in a supportive environment normalizes the fluctuations inherent to our emotional existence. Just as the Stoics teach us to accept the things we cannot control, so too can children learn to embrace their emotional landscape, understanding that joy and sorrow are both valid experiences.

Furthermore, the routine itself cultivates a sense of security and predictability. Children with SPD often thrive in structured environments, and the consistency of these check-ins can be a stabilizing anchor in their daily lives. In predictable moments, they find solace, knowing they have the space to explore their feelings without judgment.

In addition, these check-ins serve as opportunities for parents to reinforce emotional regulation strategies. By gently reminding children of tools such as deep breathing or seeking a quiet space, parents empower them to navigate overwhelming emotions with grace. This guidance is akin to the Stoic practice of preparing the mind for challenges. Children learn to equip themselves with strategies that enable them to respond thoughtfully rather than react impulsively.

Ultimately, the routine of emotional check-ins is more than a mere exercise; it is a foundation for emotional growth. It nurtures a profound understanding of oneself, instilling the wisdom that while emotions may rise and fall, the ability to observe, accept, and manage them is always within reach. Through this practice, parents and children together walk the path of emotional mastery, fostering resilience and a tranquil mind in the face of life's inevitable fluctuations.

Overcoming Emotional Roadblocks Together

Stoic Resilience in the Face of Emotional Setbacks

Emotional roadblocks are an intrinsic aspect of the human experience, particularly when navigating the complexities of raising a child with Sensory Processing Disorder (SPD). These challenges manifest as meltdowns, outbursts, and waves of frustration, each presenting a unique trial. However, the Stoic perspective reframes these emotional setbacks, viewing them not as failures but as vital opportunities for growth and resilience.

In the face of such difficulties, it is essential for parents to adopt a mindset of acceptance. Emotional setbacks are not anomalies to be avoided but rather integral components of the journey. When confronted by these moments, a Stoic response involves pausing to reflect, allowing oneself to reframe the situation. This practice transforms frustration into a valuable lesson in patience and composure.

Through this lens, parents can cultivate an environment where emotional resilience is not only encouraged but exemplified. Demonstrating this mindset teaches children that setbacks are not definitive endpoints but rather stepping stones in their development. Each emotional challenge, when approached with a Stoic attitude, becomes a chance to fortify one's character.

As both parents and children engage in this process, they gradually develop the emotional strength necessary to confront future challenges. This enduring resilience fosters a deeper bond, built on mutual understanding and shared experiences. In embracing the Stoic philosophy, both parent and child learn that the journey may be fraught with obstacles, but it is precisely through these trials that they forge a path toward greater emotional fortitude.

Building a Family Culture of Emotional Support

Building a family culture of emotional support is essential for nurturing resilience within the household. This endeavor transcends individual effort; it thrives within the collective spirit of the family. In a family where emotional support and understanding are integral, a robust foundation is laid for confronting and coping with sensory challenges.

In homes with children experiencing Sensory Processing Disorder, emotional support manifests as an affirmation of feelings, a source of comfort, and a safe haven for emotional expression. This environment fosters a sense of belonging and understanding, allowing children to voice their experiences without fear of judgment. When emotions are validated, children feel less isolated in their struggles, knowing their feelings are recognized and accepted.

Parents play a pivotal role in cultivating emotional resilience. By encouraging open dialogue about emotions, they create pathways for children to express their thoughts and feelings freely. Celebrating even the smallest victories reinforces a sense of achievement, instilling confidence in the face of challenges. Empathy becomes a guiding principle; when emotional hurdles arise, parents who respond with understanding help their children navigate these moments with grace and assurance.

A culture of emotional support teaches family members that emotions are not merely to be endured but acknowledged and managed. In this nurturing environment, children learn to harness their feelings, developing skills that will serve them throughout life. Parents who consistently provide emotional backing during trying times foster trust and confidence in their children. This unwavering support equips children with the tools they need to face the complexities of Sensory Processing Disorder, knowing they have a solid foundation of emotional understanding and resilience to rely upon.

Thus, a family that embraces emotional support cultivates an atmosphere where each member can thrive, fortified by mutual understanding and compassion. In this shared journey, resilience is not just a personal attribute; it becomes a collective strength, empowering the family to face life's challenges together.

The Role of Communication in Emotional Healing
Communication serves as an essential bridge in the journey of emotional healing, particularly for children grappling with sensory processing difficulties. These children often navigate a world that feels overwhelming, where their feelings may become tangled in a web of sensory input. In such situations, the capacity for clear and compassionate communication becomes paramount.

Parents must cultivate an environment of active listening, a skill that extends beyond mere words. It demands an awareness of both verbal and non-verbal signals that a child may convey. The subtleties of body language, facial expressions, and even silence can reveal profound insights into a child's emotional state. By employing open-ended questions, caregivers invite children to articulate their experiences, fostering a sense of agency and understanding.

Presence is a powerful form of communication. Simply being there, offering empathy and understanding, creates a safe space for children to explore their feelings. This attentive engagement not only facilitates emotional expression but also nurtures trust, an essential component in any healing process. Children are more likely to seek help and communicate their struggles when they feel understood and accepted.

Furthermore, effective communication aids in resolving the inevitable misunderstandings that arise from sensory sensitivities. When a child exhibits a strong reaction to a texture or sound, it is not merely a moment of distress but an opportunity for dialogue. By calmly discussing the incident afterward, parents can help their children make sense of their experiences. This reflective practice serves to demystify their reactions and equips them with strategies to navigate similar challenges in the future.

Through the lens of stoicism, it becomes clear that emotional regulation is not merely a reaction to external events but a skill that can be cultivated. Open communication plays a crucial role in this development, as it allows children to articulate their feelings, identify triggers, and explore coping mechanisms. In this way, the practice of communication does not just heal but empowers, enabling children to face the world with greater resilience and clarity.

The role of communication in emotional healing cannot be overstated. It fosters an environment of trust, encourages emotional expression, and supports the development of vital skills necessary for navigating a complex sensory world. Through dedicated and mindful communication, parents provide their children with the tools to understand and manage their emotions, paving the way for a more balanced and serene existence.

Five

Focus on What You Can Control

"We cannot choose our external circumstances, but we can always choose how we respond to them." – **Epictetus**

Focusing on What's in Our Control

The Dichotomy of Control

The practice of distinguishing between what is within our control and what lies beyond it is essential for cultivating a life of tranquility. In the realm of parenting, particularly when faced with the complexities of a child with Sensory Processing Disorder (SPD), this dichotomy becomes not just a principle, but a guiding philosophy.

In the face of challenges that arise from a child's sensory sensitivities, it is natural to feel frustration over circumstances that escape our influence. However, Stoicism teaches us to redirect our focus. We possess the capacity to control our thoughts, emotions, and actions, and this is where our energy must be invested. By acknowledging that the external triggers—a loud noise, an overwhelming crowd—are beyond our command, we liberate ourselves from the futile struggle against the uncontrollable. When confronted with a situation that causes distress, such as a sudden sound that startles our child, we must remember that our response is our own domain. Rather than allowing anxiety or irritation to take hold, we can choose to remain composed.

This choice not only serves our emotional well-being but also provides a stabilizing influence for our child. By guiding them to a quieter space, we exemplify the Stoic virtue of self-control. We do not seek to change the external circumstances but rather adjust our internal landscape. This practice fosters resilience. Accepting that we cannot remove every obstacle allows us to develop strategies to navigate them.

Each moment of challenge becomes an opportunity to refine our response and cultivate patience. We learn to create a supportive environment that acknowledges our child's needs without becoming overwhelmed by what we cannot change.Thus, the dichotomy of control serves as a constant reminder of where our focus should lie. It empowers us to confront life's unpredictability with clarity and emotional balance. In doing so, we embrace our role not as warriors against the chaos of life, but as steadfast guides for our children, navigating the tumult with grace and fortitude.

Leonardo da Vinci - Focused on What He Could Control

Leonardo da Vinci's life embodies the art of focusing on what one can control, a lesson particularly poignant for parents raising children with Sensory Processing Disorder (SPD). Da Vinci's brilliance was not solely in his artistic talent but in his relentless pursuit of knowledge and understanding. He approached his work with a sense of wonder and curiosity, allowing his interests to guide him. This flexible mindset is crucial for parents navigating the complexities of SPD, where challenges can often feel overwhelming and unpredictable.

Da Vinci's tendency to leave projects unfinished can be seen as a reflection of his deep engagement with the world around him. He prioritized exploration and learning over completion, which resonates with the idea that progress is often nonlinear, especially in the context of raising a child with SPD. For parents, this serves as a reminder that perfection is not the goal; rather, it is the journey of discovery and adaptation that truly matters.

Moreover, da Vinci's meticulous studies of anatomy highlight the importance of understanding the underlying principles of a situation. For parents, this translates into the necessity of understanding their child's unique sensory needs and responses. By focusing on what can be controlled—such as creating a supportive environment, employing effective strategies, and advocating for their child's needs—parents can foster growth and development.

Leonardo's ability to visualize concepts beyond his time reflects the imaginative thinking that can also benefit parents and children facing the challenges of SPD. It encourages parents to envision a future where their child's potential is realized, despite current difficulties. By fostering an environment rich in exploration and creativity, they can help their children express themselves and navigate their sensory experiences more effectively.

Ultimately, da Vinci teaches us that success is not defined by completed projects or societal standards but rather by the pursuit of knowledge, passion, and adaptability. For parents of children with SPD, this means focusing on incremental progress, celebrating small victories, and maintaining an unwavering commitment to understanding and supporting their child's unique journey. Embracing da Vinci's philosophy allows parents to cultivate resilience in themselves and their children, reinforcing that it is the effort and intention behind their actions that truly matter.

Letting Go of Perfectionism
Letting go of perfectionism in parenting, especially when raising a child with Sensory Processing Disorder (SPD), is an essential practice rooted in the principles of Stoicism. As parents, we often impose upon ourselves unrealistic expectations, striving for an ideal that is neither attainable nor beneficial. Stoicism teaches us to distinguish between what we can control—our actions and responses—and what we cannot—our child's unique sensory experiences and reactions. This understanding calls for a relinquishment of the need for perfection, which can be a heavy burden.

The relentless pursuit of perfection can lead to frustration and burnout, not only for ourselves but for our children as well. We may feel compelled to create an environment devoid of challenges, believing that doing so will alleviate our child's struggles. However, such an endeavor is likely to be futile. Instead of seeking to eliminate difficulties, we should cultivate patience and acceptance, recognizing that our child's sensory sensitivities are a part of their identity and development. Progress is not a straight path but a winding journey, marked by both steps forward and setbacks.

Embracing imperfections, both in ourselves and in our children, is a fundamental aspect of this Stoic approach. Mistakes—whether they manifest as a sensory meltdown or a moment of impatience—are not signs of failure but rather opportunities for reflection and growth. Each challenge we face offers a chance to learn, adapt, and respond with greater wisdom in the future. By acknowledging that perfection is an illusion, we free ourselves from the shackles of self-criticism and the unrealistic expectations we place on our children.

Shifting our focus from perfection to progress allows us to approach each situation with clarity and purpose. In doing so, we foster an environment where both we and our children can thrive. Each small improvement, each moment of understanding, and each instance of compassion becomes a testament to our commitment to growth. This journey is not about reaching an endpoint; it is about engaging fully in the process, appreciating the strides we make along the way, and understanding that true fulfillment lies in our ability to adapt and respond thoughtfully to the complexities of life.

Actionable Steps for Controlling What You Can

The practice of focusing on what we can control is essential in navigating the complexities of parenting, especially when addressing the needs of a child with sensory processing difficulties. This approach calls for deliberate action in shaping our surroundings and interactions.

Creating a sensory-friendly environment is a meaningful step. By minimizing sensory overload, such as harsh lighting and loud noises, we foster a space that allows our child to flourish. The introduction of calming tools—weighted blankets that provide a sense of security, or noise-canceling headphones to shield against overwhelming sounds—are not merely conveniences but essential instruments in cultivating a nurturing atmosphere.

Establishing predictable routines is another vital element within our sphere of influence. Children with sensory processing disorder often find solace in structure; knowing what to expect can significantly mitigate anxiety. By creating a daily framework that outlines activities and transitions, we help our child gain a sense of control over their environment, fostering confidence and reducing distress.

Moreover, the practice of self-care is a critical aspect that parents can actively manage. Taking time to replenish our emotional reserves is not an indulgence but a necessity. By maintaining clarity and calmness in challenging moments, we position ourselves to respond thoughtfully rather than react impulsively, thereby modeling resilience for our child.

In embracing these actionable steps, we lay a stable foundation that not only meets our child's sensory needs but also nurtures our own well-being. This balance is crucial; as we cultivate our inner strength and clarity, we enhance our capacity to support our child effectively. In focusing on what we can control, we embody the stoic principle of accepting what lies beyond our grasp while diligently tending to our responsibilities and environment.

Simplifying Daily Routines for Children with SPD

The Importance of Predictability

The journey of raising a child with Sensory Processing Disorder (SPD) demands an adherence to the principles of predictability and routine. Children navigating the complexities of sensory sensitivities often find themselves ensnared in a web of anxiety, particularly when confronted with the unpredictable nature of their environment. It is through the establishment of a structured daily routine that we can cultivate a sanctuary of security for them.

Consider the significance of a consistent rhythm to daily life. Mealtimes, playtimes, and bedtimes should not be mere occurrences; they must be anchors in a turbulent sea. A well-defined morning routine, wherein a child knows what to expect, serves as a grounding force that mitigates the overwhelming impact of transitions. The clarity of what comes next eases the mind and spirit, allowing the child to navigate daily challenges with greater ease.

Predictability creates a framework within which children can thrive. It is crucial to provide them with the tools to understand their day, to visualize what lies ahead. Visual schedules, adorned with pictures or symbols, serve as a map through the unpredictable landscape of life. They grant children a semblance of control, transforming what might seem chaotic into a comprehensible sequence of events.

By fostering an environment rich in routine and predictability, we not only reduce anxiety but also empower our children. They learn to prepare themselves emotionally and physically for the transitions that punctuate their day. In this way, we guide them toward resilience, equipping them with the strength to face the world, one structured moment at a time.

Managing Sensory Triggers Throughout the Day

Managing sensory triggers throughout the day requires a deliberate and composed approach. It is essential for parents to cultivate an awareness of their child's unique sensitivities, recognizing that each individual experiences the world differently. By doing so, they can create an environment that mitigates distress and fosters a sense of calm.

Adjustments to the surroundings are not merely reactive but proactive measures that embody wisdom. For instance, in the face of a child's sensitivity to loud noises, equipping them with noise-canceling headphones during outings to crowded places becomes an act of foresight. Similarly, employing soft lighting at home serves to cultivate tranquility, transforming the space into a sanctuary where the child can thrive. Such modifications, though seemingly minor, hold significant power in alleviating sensory overload, enabling the child to navigate the world with greater ease and confidence.

Yet, it is crucial to acknowledge the unpredictable nature of sensory triggers. They can emerge without warning, demanding a swift and composed response from parents. In these moments, maintaining a calm demeanor is paramount. A soothing voice, a gentle touch, or the presence of a familiar sensory tool, such as a stress ball or fidget toy, can serve as anchors that help the child regain their composure. This mindful response reflects a stoic understanding that while one cannot control every external stimulus, one can control their reaction to it.

By adopting this proactive and composed mindset, parents empower themselves in the face of sensory challenges. They recognize that their ability to manage the environment and their responses not only supports their child but also reinforces their own resilience. In this shared journey, the pursuit of harmony amidst sensory complexities becomes a testament to the strength of both parent and child, fostering a deeper connection grounded in understanding and adaptability.

Establishing Flexibility Within Routine
Routine serves as an anchor in the tumultuous seas of daily life, providing a semblance of order and predictability. Yet, within this framework, the necessity for flexibility emerges as an essential counterbalance. For parents of children with Sensory Processing Disorder (SPD), the realization that each day presents unique challenges is crucial. What may have been effective yesterday can quickly become inadequate today, and this impermanence must be embraced.

Stoicism teaches us that the only true control we possess lies in our responses to the world around us. When faced with disruptions to routine—be it an unexpected event or a shift in a child's sensory needs—parents are called to exercise Stoic acceptance. This acceptance fosters an understanding that external disturbances are beyond our influence. Instead of resisting the change, parents can choose to navigate it with composure, adjusting the day's plans with a calm demeanor. This might manifest in shortening an outing or allowing additional time for a child to recalibrate, demonstrating a profound understanding of their needs.

Incorporating flexibility within a routine not only instills a sense of security in the child but also acknowledges the fluidity of their sensory experiences. It is essential to recognize that rigid adherence to a set plan can lead to overwhelm. By intentionally building in breaks or moments of quiet reflection, parents create opportunities for sensory recovery. These pauses are not signs of weakness but rather strategic choices that honor the child's well-being.

The true art lies in finding the equilibrium between structure and adaptability. A well-defined routine can provide stability, while the capacity to pivot when necessary fosters resilience. This dual approach supports the child's evolving sensory needs, allowing them to thrive within a nurturing environment. Simultaneously, parents cultivate their own clarity and peace of mind, recognizing that life's unpredictability, rather than being a source of frustration, can be viewed as a chance for growth and understanding.

In this balanced existence, both parent and child can navigate the complexities of life with grace, grounded in the Stoic belief that while we cannot control the winds, we can adjust our sails.

"In the midst of movement and chaos, keep stillness inside of you."
- Deepak Chopra

Finding Clarity Amidst the Chaos

The Stoic Practice of Reflection

For much of my life, reflection was never on my radar. I was always in motion, always pushing forward, always working harder, telling myself that the good times would come eventually. It wasn't until later in life that I realized how misguided that mentality had been. It was all just a vicious cycle—work harder, push harder, grind it out—and all it led to was burnout. I was chasing some elusive future, hoping that if I just worked enough, something would magically click. But looking back, it was just a crock of shit. At least for me, anyway. I worked myself into the ground, thinking that forward momentum alone would get me somewhere meaningful.

I first encountered the idea of reflection during my university days. And, to be honest, it wasn't exactly presented in the most appealing way. It was all about referencing my thoughts and memories, a process that felt, frankly, ridiculous at the time. But, despite my skepticism, it provided a great starting point—a foundation for me to begin understanding the importance of looking back and assessing where I was, how I was handling life, and how it all fit together.

These days, my practice of reflection happens at the end of the day, when the kids are asleep, and my wife has gone to bed. I step outside with a glass of whisky and a cigar, allowing the calm of the evening to settle over me. In those quiet moments, I look back at the day and think about what stood out—what were the big moments? How did I handle them? How were those moments perceived by my son, my wife, my patients, or my other children? Did I handle the situation well? What could I have done better? Where did I fall short? And, most importantly, how can I use these reflections to improve as a father, husband, and person?

My outlook on life hasn't changed—time keeps moving forward, and if you're not moving with it, you're already on the back foot. So, I don't keep a diary. For some, journaling is a great way to reflect, but I'm not that dramatic about it. For me, it's about the process of getting better today than I was yesterday. It's not about perfection; it's about improvement. I want to be better than I was before, whether it's in how I handle situations, how I respond to my children, or how I connect with my wife.

FOCUS ON WHAT YOU CAN CONTROL

"Reflection isn't about perfecting your past; it's about understanding your present and making the next moment better." – The **Philosophical Dad**

A question I ask myself regularly is, "Why?" Why do I do what I do? Why do I respond in certain ways? Why do I choose temperance over justice? And, perhaps most importantly, why do I bother with any of this at all? The answer is simple: my son needs me to. That's the motivation that keeps me going, and that's all the motivation I need. If it means I sleep less some nights to prepare his schoolwork for the next day, then so be it. Because those early morning hours spent with him are some of the most rewarding moments of my day.

Reflection stands as a pillar of Stoic philosophy, offering a pathway through the tumult of daily life. Each day, as the sun sets, it invites a moment of stillness, a chance to assess the day's journey. For those navigating the complexities of raising children with Sensory Processing Disorder, this practice becomes especially vital.

In the quietude of reflection, parents can sift through the day's events, examining actions, thoughts, and emotional responses. Each moment, whether marked by triumph or challenge, holds lessons waiting to be unveiled. Identifying what transpired allows parents to recognize their own responses, acknowledging feelings of frustration or joy without judgment. In this way, reflection transforms raw experience into understanding.

As parents contemplate what went well, they can celebrate successes, however small. These moments of recognition cultivate a deeper sense of purpose, underscoring the value of their efforts. In the face of adversity, it becomes clear that perseverance and commitment—whether in guiding a child through sensory overload or fostering moments of connection—are significant. This acknowledgment serves as a reminder that every action contributes to the broader landscape of their child's development.

Moreover, reflection fosters a shift in perspective. Instead of becoming ensnared in feelings of inadequacy or disappointment, parents can embrace a mindset of growth. By recognizing patterns in their responses and the dynamics of their interactions, they gain insight into effective strategies for future encounters. This proactive approach not only alleviates emotional burdens but also empowers parents to engage with life's challenges with renewed vigor.

Ultimately, this practice of reflection grants clarity amidst chaos. It equips parents with the tools to face the uncertainties of tomorrow, grounded in the knowledge that their journey is one of continuous learning and adaptation. Each day, they rise anew, not as victims of circumstance, but as architects of their experience, ready to navigate the complexities of parenting with wisdom and resilience.

Creating Mental Space for Clear Decision-Making

Mental clarity is an essential virtue, particularly when one is faced with the demands of parenting, especially in challenging situations such as when caring for children with Sensory Processing Disorder. The chaotic nature of life can often lead to a cluttered mind, filled with stress, fatigue, and emotional turmoil. In these moments, we must remember the teachings of Stoicism, which guide us to prioritize and simplify our thoughts and actions.

To cultivate mental space, one must first identify what truly matters. This process often requires a deliberate act of letting go—relinquishing tasks that are not essential, recognizing that doing so is not a failure but an exercise in wisdom. It is vital to practice kindness towards oneself, acknowledging that the path of parenting is fraught with unpredictability. When expectations are not met, we must not dwell in frustration but instead accept these circumstances with grace.

The Stoic approach emphasizes focusing on what lies within our control. By doing so, parents can strip away the burdens of unnecessary worry, thereby clearing the fog that often clouds judgment. This clarity is not merely a luxury; it becomes a necessity, enabling one to make decisions grounded in rational thought rather than emotional upheaval.

In high-stress situations, such as when a child experiences sensory overload, the ability to maintain a clear mind is crucial. A parent who has cultivated mental space is better equipped to assess the situation with composure, allowing them to respond thoughtfully rather than react impulsively. This measured response can lead to more effective solutions, fostering a sense of stability in the midst of chaos.

Creating mental space is not a passive act; it requires discipline and intention. It is a practice that demands regular reflection and mindfulness. By prioritizing mental clarity, parents can navigate the complexities of their responsibilities with poise, ensuring that their decisions are informed and purposeful. In embracing this Stoic principle, one not only enhances their own well-being but also provides a steady foundation for their children, modeling resilience and clarity in a world that often feels overwhelming.

Learning to Trust Your Instincts

Learning to trust your instincts is an essential part of parenting children with Sensory Processing Disorder (SPD). As you engage with your child, you become increasingly aware of their unique needs and sensitivities. The journey reveals itself through the subtle expressions and behaviors they exhibit—those fleeting moments that signal distress or discomfort. This heightened awareness is not merely instinct; it is the result of careful observation and understanding, honed over time.

In the Stoic tradition, the emphasis lies on recognizing what is within our control. In this context, trusting your instincts becomes a vital exercise in self-discipline. You learn to discern between the chaos of external opinions and the quiet voice of your own judgment. The world may present a cacophony of advice and criticism, yet the Stoic parent understands that the ultimate authority on their child's needs rests within themselves.

Navigating daily life with SPD often presents a myriad of challenges. Each moment can require a decision, a reaction, or a shift in approach. It is within these moments that the practice of Stoicism can be most beneficial. By grounding yourself in the principles of reason and self-reflection, you cultivate a steadfast confidence in your ability to respond appropriately. The more you engage with these challenges, the more you reinforce your capacity to face them with equanimity.

Trusting yourself does not imply an absence of doubt; rather, it acknowledges that doubt is a natural companion on the path of growth. Each experience, whether it results in success or a misstep, serves as an opportunity for reflection and learning. This process of self-examination allows you to refine your instincts, sharpening the clarity with which you perceive your child's needs.

As you practice Stoic principles, you cultivate resilience. You learn that your instincts are not just reactions but informed responses shaped by experience. This trust in oneself empowers you to navigate the complexities of parenting with a sense of purpose. You recognize that while you may not control every aspect of your child's sensory experiences, you do possess the tools to support them effectively.

In embracing these Stoic teachings, you foster a profound sense of confidence. You become adept at reading situations, remaining calm under pressure, and making decisions that align with your values. This journey cultivates not only your ability to respond to your child but also nurtures a deeper understanding of yourself. Through this process, you embody the Stoic ideal of being a rational and composed individual, ready to face the uncertainties of parenting with grace and resilience.

Six

Cultivating Gratitude

"Gratitude is not only the greatest of virtues, but the parent of all the others." – **Marcus Tullius Cicero**

Understanding the Power of Gratitude

The Stoic Practice of Gratitude

Gratitue, within the Stoic framework, transcends mere sentiment. It emerges as a deliberate practice, a conscious choice that fortifies the mind against the trials of existence. Stoicism asserts that the cul tivation of gratitude is essential, particularly in the face of adversity. This is not an act of blind optimism but a profound acknowledgment of the interconnectedness of life's experiences. Marcus Aure lius and Seneca, among others, understood that expressing gratitude, especially during times of hardship, serves as a bulwark against de spair.

For parents navigating the complexities of raising children with Sensory Processing Disorder (SPD), the active practice of gratitude becomes an indispensable tool. In the midst of daily challenges, it is easy to become ensnared by frustration and fatigue. However, by intentionally directing attention towards the positive elements, however minor they may seem, parents can transform their perspective. This shift allows for a recognition of the small victories that punctuate each day—moments of connection, instances of growth, or fleeting periods of tranquility. Embracing gratitude does not equate to denying the existence of struggle; rather, it is an exercise in balance. It involves acknowledging the chaos while simultaneously recognizing the blessings that reside within it. On days filled with sensory overload, when the emotional landscape appears tumultuous, taking a moment to reflect on the positive aspects can be profoundly grounding.

Perhaps it is the child's discovery of a coping strategy or a shared moment of calm that stands out amidst the noise. As this practice is woven into the fabric of daily life, it nurtures emotional resilience. The act of gratitude instills a sense of perspective, reminding us that even within adversity, there are seeds of appreciation to be found. By fostering this mindset, parents not only enhance their own well-being but also model a profound lesson for their children: that even in the most challenging circumstances, there exists a pathway to peace through the recognition of life's inherent blessings.

Gratitude as a Path to Emotional Resilience

Gratitude stands as a formidable ally in the pursuit of emotional resilience. It invites us to direct our attention toward the abundance in our lives, rather than the voids we perceive. In the realm of parenting, particularly for those nurturing children with Sensory Processing Disorder, this shift is not merely beneficial; it is transformative. By embracing gratitude, parents can step away from the shadows of helplessness and frustration.

They begin to recognize the myriads of strengths present in their lives and in their children. Observing the progress their child has made, however incremental, becomes a source of strength. Each small victory is a testament to resilience, both in the child and in the parent. This perspective fosters a deeper understanding of their journey, where challenges are not mere obstacles but opportunities for growth and learning.

The support received from friends, family, and community further en riches this experience, reinforcing a sense of belonging and shared purpose. The practice of gratitude cultivates an emotional fortitude that empowers parents to confront adversity with a renewed sense of pur pose. In this way, they become not just passive recipients of circumstances but active participants in shaping their emotional landscape. The daily struggles that accompany raising a child with SPD can be daunting; however, gratitude serves to anchor them, offering a source of positivity amidst the turmoil. Regularly engaging in gratitude rewires the mind, creating a habitual lens through which one views the world. This reconditioning diminishes the grip of stress, allowing for a clearer perspective on life's demands. The emotional toll of daily challenges lessens, replaced by a resilient spirit that finds joy and meaning even in adver sity.

Moreover, this practice is not confined to the parents alone. It extends to their children, who observe and learn from the resilience modeled before them. By witnessing the transformative power of gratitude, children are equipped with tools to navigate their own challenges. They learn to seek the good in their experiences, fostering a mindset that embraces positivity and hope. In embracing gratitude, parents cultivate not only their own emotional well-being but also lay the groundwork for their chil dren's resilience. This shared journey, grounded in appreciation, becomes a guiding light through the complexities of life, illuminating the path toward a more fulfilling existence.

The Benefits of Gratitude for the Family Unit

Gratitude serves as a steadfast anchor in the tumultuous seas of family life. When gratitude is woven into the fabric of daily interactions, it cultivates a profound sense of appreciation that permeates the household. This practice does not merely benefit individual members; it transforms the family unit into a cohesive force, fostering an environment where positivity thrives. Establishing regular rituals, such as sharing expressions of gratitude during meals, can significantly reinforce family bonds. Each voice contributes to a collective acknowledgment of the good within their lives, creating a shared purpose that unites members. The act of recognizing and vocalizing gratitude cultivates an awareness of the abundance that exists even amidst challenges.

A gratitude jar, where each member deposits notes of appreciation, serves as a tangible reminder of the family's collective strengths and joys. Over time, this practice nurtures an atmosphere where emotional well-being is prioritized, and appreciation becomes a natural reflex. For families with children who experience Sensory Processing Disorder (SPD), the benefits of gratitude become even more pronounced. By fostering a culture of gratitude, parents create a space where the child with sensory sensitivities can feel grounded. This focus on gratitude encourages all family members to connect deeply, reaffirming their place within the family structure.

Children with SPD often navigate a landscape filled with overwhelming stimuli and frustrations. Encouraging them to articulate what they are thankful for can gently redirect their attention from the burdens of their sensory experiences to the positives in their lives. As children learn to express their gratitude, they gain vital tools for emotional resilience. This shift in focus teaches them to recognize their strengths and progress, even in the face of adversity. By framing their experiences in a positive light, they cultivate an inner fortitude that allows them to confront sensory challenges with a mindset that values growth and appreciation. In this way, gratitude becomes a powerful teacher, guiding children toward a balanced perspective that embraces both the trials and triumphs of their journey. Ultimately, the practice of gratitude within the family unit transcends mere acknowledgment of good fortune; it fosters a spirit of unity, resilience, and understanding, equipping each member to navigate life's complexities with a heart full of appreciation.

Teaching Gratitude to Children with SPD

The Power of Modeling Gratitude

The act of gratitude is a profound practice that resonates deeply within the human experience, particularly for children navigating the complexities of Sensory Processing Disorder (SPD). By embodying gratitude ourselves, we offer a living testament to its value. This practice is not merely a fleeting gesture; it becomes a cornerstone of our family's ethos. When we express thankfulness for the mundane—be it a shared meal, a moment of laughter, or the quiet beauty of nature—we provide our children with a framework through which they can learn to view the world. This modeling is crucial, for it serves as a guide through the often turbulent waters of their sensory experiences. When children observe their parents acknowledging the small joys even amidst adversity, they internalize the understanding that gratitude does not diminish the presence of difficulty; rather, it enhances their resilience.

In moments when sensory overwhelm threatens to engulf them, a parent's acknowledgment of both the struggle and the gratitude for the child's efforts becomes a powerful lesson. By articulating appreciation for their courage in facing these challenges, we teach our children that their journey, however fraught with obstacles, is also rich with opportunities for gratitude. They learn that while their sensitivities may set them apart, they are also part of a greater narrative that includes appreciation for the effort, growth, and love that accompanies their experiences.

Thus, by consistently integrating gratitude into our daily conversations, we cultivate an environment where it is not only understood but embraced.

This becomes an emotional vocabulary that empowers children with SPD to articulate their own feelings. Through our examples, we instill in them the wisdom that even in the midst of trials, there exists a spectrum of beauty and gratitude waiting to be recognized. In this way, we prepare them not just to endure, but to thrive, embracing every moment as a chance to find appreciation and strength.

Creating Gratitude Rituals for Children
Creating gratitude rituals for children provides a steadfast anchor in the often tumultuous sea of emotions and experiences. For children with Sensory Processing Disorder (SPD), the world can feel overwhelming, and the practice of gratitude serves as a grounding force. By establishing structured rituals, we offer these children a clear pathway to express their appreciation, transforming what may seem abstract into something tangible and relatable. A nightly practice of sharing gratitude within the family serves not only to cultivate thankfulness but also to reinforce familial bonds. Each member, regardless of age, contributes by reflecting on their day and identifying moments of appreciation.

For children, this can take the form of drawing or using symbols, allowing them to communicate their feelings in a non-verbal manner that aligns more closely with their sensory experiences. This ritual creates a safe space where gratitude is not only shared but celebrated, fostering an envi ronment of acceptance and understanding. The creation of a gratitude journal further enriches this practice. Even the youngest can engage meaningfully, whether through drawing or with the assistance of a parent in writing. This shared activity reinforces emotional literacy and provides an opportunity for parents to guide their children in recognizing the positive aspects of their lives, despite the challenges they may face due to SPD. Each try becomes a testament to resilience, a visual or written acknowledgment of the good that exists, no matter how small.

Through these rituals, children learn to identify and celebrate small victories, which cultivates a profound sense of accomplishment and well-being. The act of gratitude, rooted in daily practice, becomes a lens through which they can view their experiences. It nurtures a mindset that appreciates the present, even amidst sensory overload. In this way, gratitude rituals serve not only as expressions of thanks but as essential tools for emotional development and resilience, equipping children with the ability to find joy and meaning in their lives, regardless of their sensory challenges. Winston

Churchill – Leading Through Change During Crisis

Winston Churchill's leadership during World War II is often hailed as one of the finest examples of resilience, adaptability, and the power of emotional endurance in the face of overwhelming adversity. As Britain stood alone against the Axis powers, Churchill's unyielding spirit and flexible approach to leadership kept the nation focused on its larger goal: survival and eventual victory. Despite facing relentless challenges, including military setbacks, personal criticism, and the overwhelming nature of global conflict, Churchill's ability to adapt his strategies and remain calm in the face of change was critical to the eventual success of the Allied forces. Churchill's ability to embrace change, especially in moments of national crisis, mirrors the challenges faced by parents raising children with Sensory Processing Disorder (SPD).

Much like the fluctuating tides of wartime, the experiences of children with SPD can be unpredictable and ever-changing. Parents, like Churchill, are often faced with shifting circumstances, where one approach may work one day, but fail the next. Sensory sensitivities, emotional overload, and difficulties with social interactions can make it feel as though every day presents a new battle. Just as Churchill adapted his strategies in response to changing conditions, parents of children with SPD must continuously adjust their approach, remaining flexible and focused on the long-term goal: fostering their child's well-being and growth.

Churchill's leadership was not about avoiding change, but about understanding that change was inevitable and adapting to it. His famous speeches during the darkest times of the war—such as his "We shall fight on the beaches" address—were not just calls for courage but reflections of his ability to motivate the British people to embrace their circumstances, however dire, and to keep fighting. His approach was not just about tactical flexibility; it was about instilling a mindset of resilience in the face of the unknown. For parents, this philosophy is crucial. Embracing the challenges of SPD with an adaptable mindset is key to fostering a sense of security and stability in their child. When strategies for managing sensory overload, emotional meltdowns, or social difficulties don't work as planned, the ability to pivot and try new methods is essential. Like Churchill's ability to adapt his tactics during the war, parents must adjust their approach based on their child's evolving needs and sensory sensitivities.

"To improve is to change; to be perfect is to change often." – **Winston Churchill**

Churchill's belief in constant adaptation is a reminder for parents that perfection is not the goal—flexibility is. Embracing change means accepting that not every solution will work, but through con tinued effort and adaptability, progress can be made. Each challenge faced with SPD is an opportunity for growth, both for the child and the parent. The ability to remain calm, adjust strategies, and stay fo cused on the greater purpose—supporting the child's journey and fostering their emotional well-being—is where true resilience lies. Churchill's legacy teaches us that resilience is not simply about enduring hardship—it's about adapting to it, learning from it, and finding new ways to move forward. Similarly, parents of children with SPD can draw strength from their ability to embrace change, knowing that each day presents new opportunities to learn and grow, even when the path is uncertain.

Shifting Focus from What They Can't Do to What They

Children with Sensory Processing Disorder (SPD often find them- selves entrenched in feelings of frustration due to their perceived limitations. These limitations can manifest as difficulties in social interactions, aversions to certain textures, or an overwhelming response to sensory stimuli. In such moments, it is essential for parents to guide their children toward a more constructive perspective—one that emphasizes what they can do rather than what they cannot. When parents actively encourage this shift in focus, they provide their children with the tools to recognize and celebrate their own strengths and achievements.

Each small victory, such as remaining calm amidst the chaos or successfully employing techniques to self soothe during moments of sensory overload, deserves acknowledgment. This recognition is not merely praise; it is a cultivation of gratitude for progress, however incremental it may appear. By fostering an environment where accomplishments are celebrated, parents empower their children to view their sensory challenges through a lens of resilience and adaptability. This approach transforms obstacles into opportunities for growth, instilling a belief that every effort counts. As children learn to appreciate their own progress, they become more equipped to navigate the complexities of their sensory experiences with a sense of agency.

In this stoic journey, the focus shifts from the weight of unchangeable circumstances to the strength found in personal development. Each step taken, regardless of size, is a testament to their perseverance. By nurturing this mindset, parents lay the groundwork for their children to embrace their journey with dignity, viewing each challenge not as a barrier but as a part of a broader narrative of self-discovery and empowerment.

Turning Challenges into Opportunities for Gratitude

Re-framing Challenges Through Gratitude

Re-framing challenges through gratitude is a profound practice rooted in Stoic philosophy. In the face of adversity, one can cultivate a mindset that acknowledges the presence of difficulties while simultaneously recognizing the potential for growth and learning. For parents of children with Sensory Processing Disorder (SPD), the experiences of sensory meltdowns or social struggles may initially appear as burdens. However, through the lens of gratitude, these challenges transform into invaluable lessons.

When a child undergoes a sensory overload, it can be tempting to dwell on the chaos and discomfort. Yet, by embracing gratitude, parents can perceive this moment as an opportunity to enhance their own skills in emotional regulation. It becomes a chance to practice calming techniques not only for the child but for themselves as well. This re-framing allows parents to approach the situation with a sense of purpose, viewing it as an opportunity to cultivate patience and resilience.

Moreover, this practice extends beyond the immediate situation. By modeling this perspective, parents impart a critical life lesson to their children. They teach that challenges are not mere obstacles but rather stepping stones on the path to growth. In this way, parents can guide their children to see difficulties as opportunities for learning and adaptation, fostering resilience in the face of sensory challenges. As they navigate these experiences together, both parents and children can develop a deeper understanding of their capacities to adapt and thrive.

Life, as we all know, is full of difficult moments. There are minutes, hours, days, and sometimes weeks that test our patience, our resolve, and our spirits. It can be easy to get bogged down by the weight of these moments, to let them consume our thoughts and define our outlook on life. If we dwell on them, we inadvertently create more of them.

The reality is that our mindset isn't just a passive thought process; it is the lens through which we see and interact with the world. It shapes how we respond to challenges, and more importantly, how we raise our children to do the same. The Stoics taught us that subtle shifts in how we interpret the world and the events we experience can significantly alter not only our own journey but also the paths of those around us, especially our children. They are keen observers of how we react to life's trials, and it's in these moments that we shape their perspectives as well. In the face of hardship, the question becomes not, "Why is this happening to me?" but rather, "What can I learn from this? What positive can I find, even in the darkest moments?" Finding the silver lining in our days is about training our minds to look for what's good, even when it feels like everything is going wrong. It's about focusing on what's positive in our lives and, just as importantly, in our children's lives. Teaching them to see beyond the storm and recognize the rainbow on the other side will not only improve our own outlook but will shape how they approach challenges in the future. Our mindset becomes their road map.

The myth of Persephone offers a profound perspective on reframing challenges through gratitude. In Greek mythology, Persephone, the daughter of Demeter, was abducted by Hades and taken to the Underworld. For months, her mother searched for her in grief and despair, while the Earth was shrouded in perpetual winter. This darkness mirrored the overwhelming and seemingly unchangeable challenges we can face in our own lives. Just like how Demeter felt helpless, as parents, we sometimes feel powerless in the face of SPD challenges, unsure if things will ever change or improve. Persephone's journey, however, teaches us a crucial lesson: that hardship is not the end, but often a transformative process that ultimately leads to growth.

Persephone's eventual return to the surface each year, marking the arrival of spring, is a beautiful reminder that even the darkest moments carry within them the seeds of renewal. When Persephone returns, it is not simply a return to what was lost, but the start of something new, something vibrant, full of life. The cyclical nature of Persephone's journey reflects how, as parents, we can emerge from difficult times stronger and more equipped to handle the next challenge. Much like Persephone's return, the struggles we face with SPD may feel all-consuming in the moment, but the growth, understanding, and resilience that arise from these moments can create a renewed sense of purpose and clarity in our lives. Even when things seem at their darkest, there is always a possibility of renewal, growth, and improvement.

This myth teaches us that the hard times—though inevitable—are not the end of the story. It is in our ability to adapt, reflect, and find meaning in these experiences that we transform them from burdens into opportunities for growth. When facing sensory overload, emotional meltdowns, or the overwhelming complexities of SPD, it's essential to recognize that just like Persephone's return to the surface, there will be moments of respite, moments of progress, and moments of joy. The key is to trust in the cyclical process of growth—knowing that no matter how difficult today may seem, a new chapter, a brighter moment, is always just around the corner.

"Even when the world feels heavy with struggle, the key to moving forward lies in recognizing the light that follows. Embrace the darkness, for it is what makes the light all the more precious." - **The Philosophical dad**

In the context of parenting, we can model this mindset for our children. Instead of focusing solely on the difficulties they experience, we can teach them to look for the silver linings—the moments of growth, the small victories that are often overshadowed by larger challenges. Just as Persephone's journey wasn't without its darkness, but ultimately led to renewal, we too can find the strength to face our struggles and embrace the growth that follows. This mindset—one that sees hardship as part of the journey, not as the end of it—helps us stay resilient and optimistic, even in the face of adversity.

In moments of hardship, it's crucial to remember that even when everything feels like it's falling apart, there is always something to hold onto. Just as Persephone found light in the darkness of the Underworld, so too can we find light in the chaos of our daily challenges. By embracing these moments of struggle and practicing gratitude for the lessons they bring, we teach our children how to navigate their own challenges with resilience and hope. Ultimately, reframing the challenges we face through the lens of gratitude transforms them into opportunities for growth—both for us as parents and for our children.

Gratitude for the Journey

Gratitude for the journey is a profound acknowledgment of the path that unfolds in the raising of a child with Sensory Processing Disorder (SPD). This journey is laden with trials that test the limits of endurance and understanding, yet it is also a fertile ground for growth and introspection. Parents are called to recognize that these challenges are not mere obstacles; they are integral to both the child's development and their own evolution.

In this pursuit of gratitude, one must not shy away from the difficulties faced. Instead, there lies a noble opportunity to embrace these hardships as teachers. Each moment of frustration or confusion can illuminate the depths of patience, urging parents to cultivate a steadiness of spirit. In learning to navigate their child's unique needs, they deepen their understanding, not only of their child but of the human condition itself.

Moreover, the necessity of developing coping strategies fosters resilience. Each strategy learned is a tool added to a parent's arsenal, equipping them to face not just the immediate challenges but life's broader adversities. This journey, with all its unpredictable turns, serves as a reminder that life is not solely defined by ease and comfort. The richness of experience often resides in the struggle, and the development of character is forged in adversity. Thus, the practice of gratitude transforms the perspective of parents. By choosing to focus on the lessons learned rather than solely on the trials endured, they can cultivate a mindset of appreciation for the entire experience. It is within this framework that joy can be discovered, even amid the most daunting challenges. Gratitude becomes a lens through which the journey is viewed, revealing that every step taken, regardless of its nature, contributes to a tapestry of profound meaning. Embrace this journey, for it is not a solitary path but a shared odyssey filled with connection. Each interaction with the child carries weight and significance, a bond that deepens through shared struggles and triumphs.

 The act of raising a child with SPD tran scends mere duty; it becomes a sacred endeavor where love and re silience intertwine. In fostering gratitude for this journey, parents can find solace in the knowledge that they are participants in a greater narrative. They are not defined solely by the challenges faced but are enriched by the wisdom gained and the love shared. This journey is indeed worthwhile, a testament to the strength of the human spirit and the profound beauty that arises from embracing both the light and the shadow.

Seven

Embracing Change

"The more a man knows, the more he realizes he doesn't know."
– Socrates

The Nature of Change and Its Role in Parentin

Understanding the Constant Nature of Change

One must recognize that change is an inherent aspect of existence. In the realm of parenting, particularly when guiding a child with Sensory Processing Disorder (SPD), this understanding becomes profound. The world is in a state of flux, and so too are the experiences of our children. Their sensory sensitivities and emotional reactions are not static; they morph and evolve in ways that can feel bewildering.

To embrace change is to accept the reality that each day may present unforeseen challenges and opportunities. Stoicism teaches us that it is not the external circumstances that dictate our emotional state, but our responses to them. As parents, we encounter a myriad of shifting dynamics—behavioral patterns, emotional needs, and developmental stages. Acknowledging this fluidity allows us to foster resilience within ourselves and our children.

Resisting change often leads to frustration and despair, as we grapple with what cannot be controlled. Instead, we must cultivate an attitude of acceptance, recognizing that every moment of discomfort is a chance for growth. By adapting our expectations and being willing to modify our approaches, we create an environment conducive to exploration and understanding.

Flexibility becomes our ally. It is essential to adapt routines and find new coping strategies that align with our child's current state. What may have worked yesterday may no longer suffice today. This does not signify failure; rather, it is an invitation to engage more deeply with our child's needs. Stoicism encourages us to remain steadfast in our purpose while fluid in our methods.

Embracing change does not mean surrendering to chaos; it means actively participating in the unfolding of life. It calls for a calm center amid the storms of uncertainty, where we can maintain clarity of thought and purpose. By relinquishing the need for rigid control, we allow ourselves and our children the freedom to navigate their experiences with grace and adaptability. In doing so, we not only support their journey but also nurture our own emotional wellbeing.

Parenting as an Adaptive Process

Parenting a child with Sensory Processing Disorder (SPD) embodies the essence of adaptability. Each day unfolds with its own set of trials, and solutions that proved effective yesterday may falter today. Embracing the Stoic perspective, we recognize that our capacity to adapt is not merely a function of circumstance but a profound strength. The Stoic principle encourages us to concentrate on what lies within our control—our thoughts, actions, and responses. In doing so, we fortify ourselves against the inevitable uncertainties that accompany parenting.

When faced with the frustration of plans unraveling, we must cultivate the ability to step back and reflect. This moment of pause allows us to reassess and recalibrate our approach. In the realm of parenting a child with SPD, flexibility is paramount. These children flourish in environments that are predictable and structured; however, they also require a degree of adaptability to meet their fluctuating sensory needs. This duality demands that we, as parents, be both steadfast and pliable.

The journey of parenting is not solely about managing the external landscape; it is equally about the evolution of our inner mindset. We must cultivate a willingness to relinquish rigid expectations and acknowledge that there is no universal blueprint for raising a child with SPD. Each day presents a unique canvas upon which we must paint our responses, guided by an open mind attuned to our child's evolving needs.

This adaptability fosters a sense of calm and focus within us, a necessary antidote to the chaos that can arise from unexpected challenges. By embracing the Stoic ideal of resilience, we equip ourselves to navigate the complexities of parenting with grace. We learn to view setbacks not as failures but as opportunities for growth, both for ourselves and our children. In this way, we foster an environment that nurtures their development and empowers us to meet the demands of our role with wisdom and fortitude.

Building Resilience Through Flexibility

Building resilience through flexibility is an endeavor that demands our attention and commitment. As parents, our ability to adapt in the face of change serves not only as a personal strength but also as a vital lesson for our children. By embracing the inevitability of change, we cultivate a mindset that views difficulties not as insurmountable barriers but as opportunities for growth and development.

When children observe us confronting challenges with patience and adaptability, they internalize these behaviors. They learn that resilience is not an inherent trait but a skill that can be developed. This is particularly significant for children with Sensory Processing Disorder (SPD), who often encounter unexpected sensory stimuli that can disrupt their sense of stability. For them, resilience becomes a necessary tool, enabling them to navigate their unique challenges with courage and creativity.

As parents, we play a crucial role in this process. By fostering an environment that encourages experimentation and exploration, we provide our children with the freedom to test their limits and discover their capabilities. It is essential to create a safe space where they can process their experiences and emotions, allowing them to build confidence in their ability to adapt.

Resilience through flexibility is not merely about enduring hardships; it is about flourishing amidst them. When we approach life's challenges with a stoic mindset, recognizing that adversity is part of the human experience, we model a profound truth for our children: that they too can emerge stronger from their trials. This perspective transforms the parent-child relationship, reinforcing bonds of trust and mutual understanding.

In this way, each challenge becomes a stepping stone toward greater resilience. As we practice patience and adapt to changing circumstances, we create a positive feedback loop that benefits both us and our children. Together, we learn to embrace uncertainty and cultivate stability within ourselves and our family. This shared journey enhances our connection and instills a lasting sense of security, reminding us that even in the face of unpredictability, we can thrive through resilience and flexibility.

Helping Children with SPD Navigate Change

Preparing Children for Transitions

Helping children with Sensory Processing Disorder (SPD) navigate change is an endeavor rooted in the Stoic recognition of the inevitability of transition. Life, by its very nature, is a series of transformations. The Stoic philosophy encourages us to accept this reality, understanding that resistance to change often leads to unnecessary suffering. For children with SPD, who may experience heightened anxiety during transitions, preparedness becomes a vital tool in fostering resilience.

To aid children in navigating changes, it is essential to engage in open discussions about what lies ahead. Anticipating transitions allows both parents and children to confront the unknown with clarity. By employing visual schedules or cues, parents create a tangible framework that helps children grasp the sequence of events, reducing uncertainty and fostering a sense of control over their environment. This practice not only provides security but also empowers children to embrace the changes, knowing they are equipped to face them.

Consider the transition from a serene, quiet home setting to the bustling atmosphere of a family gathering. Acknowledging this shift in advance, parents can demystify the experience by discussing what to expect. Sharing coping strategies, such as using noise-canceling headphones or identifying quiet spaces for respite, instills confidence in children. These tools serve as reminders that while they may encounter discomfort, they possess the means to navigate through it.

By normalizing transitions, parents reinforce the Stoic principle that change is an inherent part of life. This acceptance does not mean passivity; instead, it encourages proactive engagement. The emotional resilience built during these preparations is invaluable, as it equips children to face future changes with greater fortitude. Each transition becomes an opportunity for growth, teaching them that while they cannot control the circumstances, they can control their responses.

In guiding children with SPD through life's inevitable changes, we cultivate not only their adaptability but also their understanding of the world around them. Embracing change, rather than fearing it, lays the foundation for a life rich in experience and growth, aligned with the tenets of Stoicism.

Building Emotional Flexibility

Emotional flexibility is crucial for navigating the complexities of life, especially for children with Sensory Processing Disorder (SPD). These children often struggle to process sensory information, which can lead to heightened emotional responses. When faced with sensory overload or unexpected changes, their emotions can become intense and difficult to manage. This is where the concept of emotional flexibility becomes vital. It involves the capability to adapt one's emotional responses in light of shifting circumstances and stimuli.

Stoicism offers valuable insights into how to cultivate this emotional flexibility. By promoting a mindset of emotional detachment from external events, Stoicism encourages individuals to focus on their internal responses rather than being swept away by the chaos of the outside world. For children with SPD, this can serve as a foundational principle. Parents can support their children by helping them recognize and label their feelings, which is the first step toward understanding and managing those emotions.

Implementing self-regulation techniques is essential in this process. Simple practices like deep breathing can be incredibly effective. Teaching deep breathing exercises allows children to take a moment to pause and regain control. Mindfulness practices can also provide tools for staying grounded, enabling children to observe their thoughts and feelings without judgment. Creating a calm-down corner at home can serve as a safe space where children can retreat when emotions become overwhelming, allowing them to practice self-soothing strategies.

As children learn to navigate their emotions more effectively, they begin to grasp a critical life lesson: emotions are temporary and manageable. This understanding fosters resilience, equipping them to handle life's inevitable challenges with greater ease. Over time, children with SPD can become increasingly adept at adjusting their emotional responses to their environments. They learn to exercise self-control, which not only aids in their personal development but also enhances their emotional intelligence.

By nurturing emotional flexibility, parents empower their children to face difficulties with confidence and poise. This journey is not just about managing emotions; it is about instilling a sense of agency in children, helping them realize that while they may not control their external circumstances, they can govern their internal state. This shift in perspective is transformative, paving the way for healthier emotional experiences and stronger coping mechanisms in the face of adversity.

Accepting the Impermanence of Sensory Experiences

Life, as we all know, is full of difficult moments. There are minutes, hours, days, and sometimes weeks that test our patience, our resolve, and our spirits. It can be easy to get bogged down by the weight of these moments, to let them consume our thoughts and define our outlook on life. If we dwell on them, we inadvertently create more of them. The reality is that our mindset isn't just a passive thought process; it is the lens through which we see and interact with the world. It shapes how we respond to challenges, and more importantly, how we raise our children to do the same.

The Stoics taught us that subtle shifts in how we interpret the world and the events we experience can significantly alter not only our own journey but also the paths of those around us, especially our children. They are keen observers of how we react to life's trials, and it's in these moments that we shape their perspectives as well. In the face of hardship, the question becomes not, *"Why is this happening to me?"* but rather, *"What can I learn from this? What positive can I find, even in the darkest moments?"*

Finding the silver lining in our days is about training our minds to look for what's good, even when it feels like everything is going wrong. It's about focusing on what's positive in our lives and, just as importantly, in our children's lives. Teaching them to see beyond the storm and recognize the rainbow on the other side will not only improve our own outlook but will shape how they approach challenges in the future. Our mindset becomes their roadmap.

A great example of this concept comes from the mythical tale of the *Phoenix*. In various mythologies, the Phoenix is a bird that bursts into flames, only to be reborn from its ashes. This continuous cycle of destruction and rebirth symbolizes renewal and the impermanence of all things. The Phoenix rises again, stronger and more vibrant than before, representing the idea that even in our most difficult, chaotic moments, there's always potential for growth and transformation.

> *"Life is a series of moments—some stormy, some calm—but the key to resilience is not in avoiding the storms, but in learning how to rise after the rain has passed."* – **The Philosophical Dad**

Much like the Phoenix, sensory overload and other intense experiences in our lives can feel all-consuming, but they are temporary. Just as the Phoenix rises from the ashes, we too can emerge stronger and more grounded after the storm. The challenges we face—whether they are sensory overload or any other trial—don't define us. It's how we handle those moments, how we respond and adapt, that shapes our journey. And as parents, the ability to navigate these moments with calm and clarity not only helps us but also teaches our children how to weather their own storms.

As we embrace the Stoic principle of adaptability, we begin to see that everything is impermanent, including the overwhelming moments we experience with our children. The key is in accepting that impermanence, knowing that just as the Phoenix rises again, so too will we find peace and strength once the chaos has passed. It's not about avoiding the storms, but about learning how to rise from them, stronger and more resilient than before.

Sensory processing challenges can create a profound sense of overwhelm in children, making the world feel like an unyielding storm of sensations. Yet, as Stoicism teaches, all things are transient, including our discomforts. It is essential for children to grasp that the intense moments of sensory overload are not permanent fixtures in their lives but fleeting experiences that will inevitably pass.

Parents play a pivotal role in guiding their children through these tumultuous times. By imparting the wisdom of impermanence, they can help their children cultivate a sense of resilience. When faced with overwhelming sensations, a gentle reminder that these feelings are temporary can serve as a grounding force. This understanding fosters a healthier perspective, transforming panic into acceptance.

The very essence of Stoicism lies in the recognition that change is an inherent part of existence. Each sensory experience, whether pleasurable or distressing, is but a moment in the continuum of life. By instilling this awareness, parents can empower their children to see beyond the immediate discomfort, offering them the tools to cope with and manage their reactions.

As children begin to internalize the notion that discomfort is not an enemy to be feared but a passing visitor, they discover a newfound confidence in their ability to navigate change. This shift in perspective not only alleviates anxiety but also reinforces their agency in the face of adversity. They learn to embrace the unpredictability of life, understanding that the ability to adapt is one of their greatest strengths.

In accepting the impermanence of sensory challenges, children move toward a more profound acceptance of life's inherent fluctuations. They become warriors of their own experiences, equipped to face the world with a steady heart and a clear mind. Thus, the practice of recognizing that all sensations, both joyful and overwhelming, are temporary enables children to forge a path of empowerment and resilience amidst the chaos.

The Stoic Approach to Managing Uncertainty

Viktor Frankl – Finding Meaning in the Midst of Suffering

Viktor Frankl's journey is a profound reminder of the strength of the human spirit in the face of unimaginable suffering. As a psychiatrist and Holocaust survivor, Frankl lived through horrors that most of us can scarcely comprehend. He spent years in Nazi concentration camps during World War II, enduring physical and emotional torment. But despite the brutality and loss that surrounded him, Frankl's ability to adapt—his ability to maintain his psychological and emotional stability—became the foundation for his groundbreaking work in psychology and the development of logotherapy.

Frankl's belief was simple, yet powerful: even in the darkest of times, we have the ability to choose how we respond. The external world, with all its cruelty and pain, was beyond his control, but his internal world—his mindset, his perspective—remained his to shape. As Frankl wrote, *"When we are no longer able to change a situation, we are challenged to change ourselves."* His strength didn't come from physical power, but from his ability to find meaning in his suffering. He discovered that those who survived the most unbearable conditions weren't necessarily the strongest physically, but those who could find a purpose within their suffering. For Frankl, that purpose was clear: to survive, to share his story, and to help others find their own meaning in life, no matter their circumstances.

This narrative resonates deeply with the journey of parents raising children with Sensory Processing Disorder (SPD). Much like Frankl, parents of children with SPD are forced to adapt continuously, adjusting their strategies and responses as their child's needs evolve. SPD doesn't follow a predictable pattern—it brings sensory overload, emotional meltdowns, and social difficulties, all of which can leave both parents and children feeling overwhelmed. There are days when the path forward is unclear, and solutions don't come easily. Yet, like Frankl, parents can find meaning in the journey itself. By focusing on the long-term goal of supporting their child's growth and development, even small victories become meaningful steps forward.

Frankl's words in *Man's Search for Meaning* remind us of a powerful Stoic truth: what matters most isn't the circumstances we find ourselves in, but how we choose to respond. Parents may not be able to control the sensory experiences their children face, but they can control how they react to those experiences. Whether it's managing the chaos of a sensory overload or finding new ways to support their child emotionally, parents can create an environment that fosters growth, resilience, and emotional well-being.

Just as Frankl's ability to adapt and find purpose within the unimaginable suffering of the Holocaust kept him grounded, parents of children with SPD can embrace change, adjust their approach, and find purpose in each moment. There will be setbacks, and there will be times when things feel uncertain. But by maintaining focus on the overarching goal—helping their child grow and thrive—parents can discover meaning in the journey, no matter how challenging it may be.

Frankl's experience teaches us a vital lesson: while we cannot control the external world, we always have the power to control our response. Embracing adaptability and resilience, parents can create a nurturing, supportive environment that helps their child navigate life's complexities, even when the way forward isn't always clear. Frankl's life reminds us that, through purpose and meaning, we can face even the most daunting challenges with strength and grace.

Focusing on What We Can Control

Focusing on what we can control is a cornerstone of Stoic philosophy, especially when faced with the uncertainty that often accompanies parenting a child with sensory processing difficulties. The world is inherently unpredictable, filled with unforeseen circumstances that can disrupt our plans and expectations. In these moments, Stoicism teaches us to redirect our energy towards our own thoughts and actions, recognizing that while we cannot dictate the events around us, we can choose how we respond to them.

In the realm of parenting, particularly when navigating the complexities of sensory sensitivities, it is essential to cultivate a mindset that prioritizes our internal state over external chaos. When a child encounters unexpected sensory overload—perhaps in a bustling grocery store—parents are confronted with a choice. They can either succumb to frustration and anxiety over the uncontrollable environment or they can focus on their own composure and the immediate needs of their child. By anchoring their attention on their ability to remain calm, to implement coping strategies, and to find solutions in real-time, parents embody the Stoic ideal of resilience.

This practice of self-regulation not only provides a sense of personal agency but also fosters an atmosphere of stability for the child. It is in these moments of tension that the true strength of a Stoic mindset is revealed. The ability to pause, assess the situation, and respond thoughtfully can transform a potentially overwhelming experience into a manageable one. By stepping outside for a moment of fresh air or utilizing a sensory tool, parents not only address their child's immediate needs but also model a Stoic approach to adversity—embracing the challenge with grace rather than despair.

In embracing this Stoic perspective, parents cultivate a clarity that allows them to navigate uncertainty with confidence. They learn to differentiate between what lies within their control and what does not, allowing them to conserve their energy for the aspects they can influence. This clarity not only empowers parents but also serves as a guiding light for their children, instilling in them the understanding that while the world may be unpredictable, their reactions and strategies can remain steadfast. Thus, in the face of uncertainty, the Stoic approach offers a pathway to peace, resilience, and the nurturing of a supportive environment for both parent and child.

The Role of Reflection in Adapting to Change

Reflection serves as a profound mechanism through which individuals, particularly parents, can cultivate resilience in the face of change. In a world marked by unpredictability, the Stoic practice of reflection invites one to pause and examine experiences with a discerning eye. After a challenging day, it is prudent for parents to engage in this introspective process, considering both successes and missteps.

By reflecting on what transpired, parents can discern the elements that contributed positively to their outcomes and those that fell short of expectations. This practice fosters a deeper understanding of their actions, promoting an awareness of the factors that influence their responses to challenges, such as sensory processing difficulties.

In moments of chaos, when the demands of parenting become overwhelming, it is easy to react instinctively rather than thoughtfully. Through reflection, parents can analyze instances where their strategies may have faltered. If a coping mechanism proved ineffective during a sensory overload episode, it is essential to contemplate the reasons behind its failure. Was the approach misaligned with the child's needs? Did external circumstances contribute to the ineffectiveness?

Such inquiries not only illuminate areas for improvement but also empower parents to innovate and adapt their strategies moving forward. This iterative process of learning from experience fosters a mindset rooted in growth and adaptability, essential qualities in navigating the ever-changing landscape of parenting.

Moreover, reflection allows for the cultivation of a more resilient mindset. Rather than becoming disheartened by setbacks, parents can embrace them as opportunities for learning. This Stoic perspective encourages individuals to accept the transient nature of challenges, recognizing that they are but moments in the larger journey of growth.

In embracing reflection, parents fortify themselves against the turbulence of uncertainty. They develop a keen awareness of their capabilities and limitations, enabling them to approach each new situation with greater clarity and purpose. Ultimately, reflection not only enhances their ability to manage present challenges but also equips them to face future changes with a sense of equanimity and resolve.

Trusting in the Process

Trust in the process of life is a cornerstone of Stoic philosophy. It invites us to embrace the unfolding of events with a calm and measured perspective, understanding that the journey itself is often more significant than the destination. When raising a child with Sensory Processing Disorder, this principle becomes especially vital. The path of growth may be fraught with obstacles, and the pace of progress may seem agonizingly slow. Yet, it is precisely in these moments of uncertainty that the Stoic mindset proves invaluable.

Rather than fixating on immediate results, we are reminded to appreciate the small, incremental advancements that occur along the way. Each small step taken by a child, no matter how seemingly insignificant, is part of a broader tapestry of development. Acknowledging these moments fosters a sense of peace, allowing parents to detach from the anxiety that often accompanies expectations of rapid change. This detachment does not equate to indifference; rather, it signifies a deep commitment to the process itself, where effort and perseverance become the true measures of success.

In maintaining this focus on consistent effort, parents cultivate resilience within themselves. They recognize that the journey is inherently unpredictable and that the only thing within their control is their response to the circumstances they face. This understanding not only alleviates stress but also empowers parents to remain steadfast in their commitment to their child's well-being.

Additionally, modeling this trust in the process becomes a profound lesson for the child. When parents demonstrate patience and a belief in gradual improvement, they instill a sense of hope and determination. Children learn that challenges are not insurmountable barriers but rather gateways to learning and growth. They begin to understand that mastery over their environment and themselves is a gradual journey, marked by practice and persistence. This knowledge equips them with skills to navigate life's complexities, fostering a mindset that embraces both the struggles and the triumphs.

In essence, trusting in the process transforms the experience of raising a child with SPD from one of frustration to one of purpose. It reminds us that every effort, every moment of patience, and every small success is a crucial element of a larger narrative. By embracing this Stoic approach, we not only nurture our children but also cultivate a sense of inner peace and resilience that will serve us well throughout our lives.

Eight

The Power of Reflection

"The unexamined life is not worth living." – **Socrates**

The Stoic Practice of Reflection

The Role of Reflection in Stoicism

Reflection is a cornerstone of Stoic philosophy. It is in the act of reflection that we find the means to cultivate wisdom and virtue. The great Stoics—Marcus Aurelius, Epictetus, and Seneca—recognized that without reflection, we drift aimlessly through life, governed by external circumstances rather than our rational nature. In their writings, they consistently emphasized the necessity of daily reflection as a tool to evaluate our thoughts, actions, and experiences.

In the face of life's inevitable challenges, reflection becomes a powerful ally. It enables us to understand our responses and the underlying values that drive them. For parents of children with Sensory Processing Disorder (SPD), the practice of reflection becomes particularly vital. It offers a structured moment to pause amidst the chaos and assess their handling of difficult situations, such as a sensory overload episode or a challenging transition. This deliberate examination of past experiences allows for the identification of areas needing improvement while reinforcing positive actions that foster growth.

By engaging in reflection, we shift from a reactive state—where emotions and impulses govern our actions—to a more mindful, proactive approach. This shift is essential for personal development and for nurturing our children. The Stoics engaged in self-examination through practices such as journaling or meditation, dedicating time at the day's end to review their actions and thoughts with honesty and clarity.

For parents, this practice need not be elaborate. It can be as simple as taking a few moments each evening to contemplate the day's events. What went well? What could have been handled differently? This honest self-reflection nurtures self-awareness, which is crucial for emotional resilience. It equips us to approach the following day with a clearer mind and a more positive outlook. Through the lens of reflection, we learn from every experience, transforming challenges into opportunities for growth. Thus, we embody the Stoic ideal, becoming not just better parents but wiser individuals, capable of facing the complexities of life with equanimity and grace.

Learning from Mistakes and Successes

As I step into my new role as my son's prep teacher, I'm reminded daily of the profound truth that learning from mistakes is now my new normal. Never in a million years did I imagine I would find myself in this role. I am an Osteopath, after all, and I've spent the last five years teaching graduate students—an experience I've enjoyed immensely. But teaching young children, especially my own son, Henry, is a whole different ballgame. It's a sharp learning curve, one that I'm diving into headfirst because, quite simply, it's for him. Every day is a learning opportunity, both for him and for me.

We're now four weeks into this term, and while it's tedious at times and we definitely have our ups and downs, I learn more each day about how to engage with Henry. And with that learning, our relationship has blossomed beyond what I could have imagined. It's become stronger, more meaningful, and deeper. We've entered a space of mutual understanding, where I begin to see things from his perspective and he begins to trust me more as his teacher and father.

The hard part, though, is that everything is on Henry's time. This doesn't always fit neatly with my work life, but I do my best to make it work. The key I've learned is to make sure that when he's ready to engage, I'm ready to meet him where he's at. It's not about forcing him into a structure or timeline that works for me. Instead, I've learned to weave lessons into our downtime, slipping in what we're learning into his games, allowing him to engage with it or not—there's no pressure. History has shown me that pushing too hard will only push him away. Patience is everything.

The change in our relationship has been nothing short of dramatic. We've always been close, but this journey—this new role I've taken on—has deepened our connection in ways I couldn't have foreseen. The Stoic principles I've worked to integrate into my own life have rippled out into our relationship, creating a stronger, more secure bond. There's now a deep understanding between us. We know each other's responses to actions, and we've learned how to navigate the ups and downs with more grace and less frustration. It's taken time to get here, but the work has been more than worth it.

In all of this, I've come to see that learning from mistakes, whether mine or Henry's, is the essence of growth. It's not about getting everything right the first time or avoiding mistakes. It's about reflecting on what didn't work, adjusting, and trying again. This process of reflection, both personal and shared with my son, has helped us build something far more meaningful than just academic knowledge. It's helped us build trust, patience, and understanding—qualities that will last long beyond the classroom.

"Mistakes are not failures; they are simply signposts on the road to becoming who we are meant to be. Every misstep is an opportunity to learn and grow, both as a parent and as a person." – **The Philosophical Dad**

This idea of perseverance and learning through reflection mirrors the journey of Odysseus' Return Home in Greek mythology. Odysseus, after the Trojan War, embarks on a long and treacherous journey to return home to Ithaca. His path is filled with challenges, mistakes, and obstacles, each one seemingly more insurmountable than the last. Yet, through it all, he learns valuable lessons. He faces setbacks—his shipwrecks, the Cyclops, the Sirens—but every mistake, every failure teaches him something new. His journey is a long, drawn-out process of reflection, adaptation, and personal growth.

Much like Odysseus, the journey we undertake as parents is full of detours and mistakes. But with each misstep, we learn and grow, ultimately leading us back to our own version of "home." For me, that home is the deeper connection and understanding I now have with my son. Just as Odysseus adapts to his circumstances and learns from each new challenge, I too learn from my mistakes, adjust my approach, and move forward with renewed clarity.

Learning from mistakes and successes requires a balanced perspective, one that does not shy away from the full spectrum of human experience. Reflection serves as a powerful tool for parents, enabling them to evaluate both their triumphs and shortcomings with equanimity. The Stoic philosophy teaches that neither success nor failure is the end, but rather integral parts of a continuous journey toward self-improvement.

When reflecting on successes, it is essential to recognize the actions and decisions that led to positive outcomes. For instance, when a parent successfully aids a child in navigating a sensory challenge, it is important to analyze what strategies were employed and how they contributed to that success. This reflection reinforces effective behaviors and cultivates a deeper understanding of one's strengths. The Stoic view encourages the acknowledgment of these victories not as points of pride, but as lessons that can be carried forward into future interactions, fostering resilience and wisdom.

Conversely, examining mistakes should not be a source of despair but an opportunity for growth. A Stoic approach advocates for a dispassionate analysis of what went wrong, free from harsh self-judgment. A parent might contemplate a difficult day marked by a sensory overload episode, recognizing that their response could have been more measured. Instead of wallowing in regret, they can ask themselves critical questions: "What could I have done differently?" or "What insights can I derive from this experience?" Such inquiries encourage a mindset focused on improvement rather than self-blame.

In this vein, reflection offers parents the chance to process emotions and challenge their habitual responses. By understanding the underlying causes of their reactions, they can approach similar situations with greater clarity and intention. The Stoic practice of journaling or meditative thought can provide the necessary space to engage with these reflections constructively. Each experience, whether a success or a setback, becomes a stepping stone toward becoming a more adept and thoughtful parent.

Ultimately, the Stoic belief in the importance of personal growth transforms the parenting journey into a continuous cycle of learning. Embracing both the victories and the failures with a sense of purpose allows for a richer, more profound engagement with the challenges of parenthood. In this way, reflection becomes not just a retrospective exercise but a proactive strategy for evolving into a more skilled and compassionate guardian.

Using Reflection to Cultivate Gratitude
Reflection serves as a steadfast companion in the pursuit of gratitude, guiding us to recognize the subtle victories nestled within the fabric of our daily lives. In the tumult of parenting, it is all too easy to become ensnared by the weight of challenges, allowing them to cloud our vision. Yet, when we take a moment to pause and reflect, we find that even the smallest of triumphs can illuminate our path.

Consider the child who learns a new coping skill. This moment, perhaps overlooked in the rush of daily responsibilities, represents not only that child's growth but also the dedication and resilience that parents embody. Each step forward, no matter how minor, is a testament to the effort invested and the love that fuels this journey. By acknowledging these moments, we cultivate an appreciation for the gradual process of development, both in our children and ourselves.

In the spirit of stoicism, we recognize that our focus should not merely rest on the obstacles we encounter. Instead, we should train our minds to celebrate progress, however incremental. This shift in perspective fosters a deeper sense of gratitude, enabling us to appreciate the journey, with all its complexities, rather than fixating solely on the hardships.

As we reflect on the achievements—whether a child's mastery of a sensory tool or a moment of calm in a chaotic day—we open ourselves to the joy that resides in these experiences. This practice anchors us, reminding us that within the struggle lies the essence of growth. Through reflection, we find meaning, transforming challenges into opportunities for appreciation and resilience. In doing so, we not only enrich our own lives but also model for our children the importance of recognizing and celebrating the good amidst the trials.

*"The unexamined life is not worth living." – **Socrates***

The Benefits of Reflection for Parents of Children with SPD

Improving Emotional Regulation

Reflection serves as a powerful tool for enhancing emotional regulation among parents of children with Sensory Processing Disorder (SPD). In the face of high-stress scenarios, such as sensory meltdowns or challenging transitions, the emotional landscape can become tumultuous. By engaging in reflective practices, parents can cultivate a deeper understanding of their emotional responses. This understanding is not merely an exercise in self-examination; it is a means to recognize patterns and triggers that lead to heightened emotional reactions.

For instance, a parent may observe that feelings of overwhelm arise when their child reacts adversely to sensory stimuli. This recognition is crucial, as it opens the door to more measured responses. Through the lens of Stoicism, parents are encouraged to reflect on their emotions without judgment. This non-judgmental approach allows for a clearer comprehension of emotional states, fostering the ability to make more deliberate choices in response to challenging situations.

Moreover, reflection enables parents to identify the emotional triggers that shape their reactions. Factors such as stress or fatigue can significantly influence the capacity to remain composed during episodes of sensory overload. By acknowledging these internal influences through reflection, parents can take proactive measures to manage their emotional state. This may involve adopting relaxation techniques or simply stepping back to regroup before engaging with their child.

The cultivation of self-awareness through reflection promotes emotional resilience. It empowers parents to confront each challenge with a sense of balance and understanding, acknowledging their limitations while striving for improvement. The Stoic philosophy emphasizes the importance of recognizing what is within our control and what is not, guiding parents toward a more purposeful approach in their interactions. In doing so, they not only enhance their emotional regulation but also model the virtues of patience and composure for their children, fostering an environment of stability amidst the chaos.

Enhancing Problem-Solving Skills
Reflection serves as a powerful instrument for enhancing problem-solving skills, particularly for parents navigating the complexities of raising children. In the face of daunting challenges—such as the intricacies of a new sensory environment or the turbulence of an emotional meltdown—reflection compels parents to adopt a stance of detachment and analysis. This stoic approach encourages them to assess their responses and strategies critically, discerning what proved effective and what fell short.

In the spirit of Stoicism, it is essential to recognize that obstacles are not inherently negative. They present opportunities for growth and learning. When a parent engages in thoughtful reflection, they are not merely mulling over past events but instead cultivating a mindset that values reason and contemplation. This deliberate pause allows for clarity, enabling parents to consider alternative methods and to refine their approaches in future encounters.

Take, for instance, the common struggle of a child resisting transitions. Through the lens of reflection, a parent may uncover insights that were previously obscured by the immediacy of the situation. Perhaps they realize that a visual schedule could provide the necessary structure, or that additional warning time might ease the child's anxiety. Such realizations stem from a reflective practice that prioritizes rational thought over emotional reaction.

By consistently engaging in this reflective process, parents develop a repertoire of strategies—an arsenal of techniques that can be wielded when challenges arise. This not only fosters a sense of confidence and resourcefulness but also aligns with the stoic principle of focusing on what is within one's control. While external circumstances may be unpredictable, the ability to reflect and adapt remains firmly within the parent's dominion.

Ultimately, reflection empowers parents to navigate the unpredictable waters of child-rearing with greater equanimity. It transforms challenges into lessons, enabling the cultivation of not just effective solutions, but a more profound understanding of their child's needs and responses. In this way, reflection becomes a vital ally in enhancing both the child's well-being and the parent's capacity for wise and measured action.

Strengthening Parent-Child Relationships

Strengthening parent-child relationships requires a deliberate and thoughtful approach, one grounded in the principles of reflection and self-awareness. In the realm of parenting, the path to greater understanding is paved with the willingness to examine one's own actions and responses. This introspection allows parents to become more attuned to the needs and emotions of their children, recognizing the subtleties of their experiences.

When parents engage in reflection, they cultivate an awareness of their child's sensory sensitivities and emotional landscapes. This awareness fosters compassion, enabling parents to respond with greater sensitivity rather than frustration. For instance, in moments when a child may be overwhelmed, the act of pausing to consider their feelings rather than reacting impulsively can transform the interaction. By embracing patience, parents not only show empathy but also model resilience and understanding, essential virtues in any relationship.

Furthermore, as parents improve their self-awareness, they create an environment conducive to emotional safety and growth. This nurturing atmosphere strengthens the bonds of trust between parent and child, allowing for open communication and a deeper connection. The recognition of emotions shared during significant moments—whether in times of distress or in moments of joy—serves to deepen these ties. Comforting a child during a sensory meltdown or celebrating their achievements, no matter how small, are opportunities for parents to cultivate gratitude for the relationship they share.

Reflection on these experiences reinforces the importance of nurturing a bond that is rooted in understanding and love. This conscious effort to appreciate the journey of parenting lays the groundwork for a relationship that can withstand challenges and thrive in harmony. In essence, the stoic approach to strengthening the parent-child relationship emphasizes the virtues of patience, empathy, and gratitude, guiding parents toward a more profound and enduring connection with their children.

Albert Einstein – Reflecting on His Theory of Relativity:

Albert Einstein, one of the most influential scientists in history, is renowned for his groundbreaking contributions to physics, especially the Theory of Relativity. However, what many people may not know is that Einstein exhibited traits throughout his life that align with both Asperger's Syndrome and ADHD, though he was never formally diagnosed during his lifetime. Einstein was a late talker, struggling to communicate in his early years, which was often seen as an indication of a developmental delay. His intense focus on certain subjects and his tendency to become deeply absorbed in his work at the expense of other tasks also suggest characteristics of ADHD.

As he grew older, Einstein was known for his tendency to withdraw socially, preferring solitude to the hustle and bustle of social gatherings. This introspective quality, combined with his sharp intellectual curiosity, may reflect traits associated with Asperger's Syndrome, which often includes a deep focus on specific interests and challenges in social interactions. However, rather than hindering his success, these traits contributed to his capacity for profound reflection, concentration, and innovation. Einstein's ability to continuously reflect on and revise his own theories allowed him to make groundbreaking advancements in science, particularly his ability to think outside the conventional boundaries of established scientific thinking.

For parents of children with sensory processing disorder (SPD) or Asperger's, Einstein's life serves as a powerful reminder that self-reflection, persistence, and adaptation are integral to overcoming challenges. Just as Einstein reflected on his scientific theories, parents can use reflection to adjust their parenting strategies. In the case of SPD, reflection allows parents to understand their child's unique sensory challenges and emotional responses, helping them find ways to adapt and grow alongside their children. Similarly, Einstein's ability to persist through challenges—despite his difficulties with communication and social norms—provides a model of resilience for both parents and children facing developmental challenges.

"Insanity is doing the same thing over and over and expecting different results." - **Albert Einstein**

Ultimately, Einstein's journey shows that reflection is not only a tool for scientists or philosophers but for anyone seeking to learn, grow, and adapt. By embracing reflection, especially when faced with difficulty, we can learn from our experiences and make the necessary adjustments to continue moving forward. For parents raising children with SPD, Einstein's story is a reminder that with patience, self-awareness, and continuous reflection, great progress can be made, both personally and in the development of their child's emotional and sensory resilience.

Reflection as a Tool for Personal Growth

The Role of Reflection in Personal Development
Reflection serves as a powerful instrument in the quest for personal growth, particularly for parents navigating the complexities of raising a child with Sensory Processing Disorder (SPD). This practice transcends mere evaluation of parenting strategies; it delves into the deeper realms of emotional and psychological evolution. In the crucible of parenting a child with SPD, individuals often find themselves undergoing profound transformations. Through reflection, parents can scrutinize their reactions to the myriad challenges they face, gaining clarity on their emotional responses and mindset.

In the Stoic tradition, the examination of one's actions and beliefs is paramount. This principle can be directly applied to parenting, where the act of reflection cultivates a purposeful approach to one's role. A parent might recall a moment of crisis, perhaps during a sensory overload, and reflect on their response. Did they maintain composure? Did they display patience in the face of chaos? Such contemplations reveal not only areas of strength but also opportunities for growth.

By recognizing the progress made, parents can celebrate their development while simultaneously acknowledging the aspects that still require attention. This duality is essential; it fosters a balanced perspective that encourages continual self-improvement. The Stoic approach emphasizes the importance of resilience and adaptation, urging individuals to embrace challenges as opportunities for growth.

In this ongoing journey of self-assessment, parents not only enhance their own personal development but also positively influence their child's growth. The insights gained through reflection can lead to more thoughtful interactions, increased empathy, and an enriched understanding of the child's experiences. Ultimately, this process of reflective practice aligns with the Stoic belief that personal evolution is a lifelong endeavor, one that is integral to both individual fulfillment and the nurturing of others.

Building a Growth Mindset Through Reflection

Building a growth mindset through reflection aligns closely with the Stoic philosophy of embracing the present moment and accepting the inherent unpredictability of life. In the Stoic view, the cultivation of our abilities and responses is not merely a matter of desire but a dedication to the discipline of self-examination. Reflection serves as a mirror, allowing us to scrutinize our thoughts and actions with clarity and honesty.

For parents, particularly those navigating the complexities of raising children with Sensory Processing Disorder (SPD), the path is fraught with challenges that test one's resolve. Yet, within each challenge lies an opportunity for growth. By engaging in regular reflection, parents can identify not only their successes but also their shortcomings. This practice fosters an understanding that setbacks are not merely obstacles but integral components of the learning process.

In the face of adversity, a growth mindset empowers parents to view difficulties through a lens of potential rather than defeat. Each setback transforms into a lesson, each moment of frustration becomes a stepping stone toward greater understanding. This reframing is essential; it allows parents to maintain a sense of optimism and purpose, even when the road ahead is uncertain.

Moreover, cultivating this mindset equips parents to adapt to their child's evolving needs with grace and composure. When parents reflect on their experiences, they build a reservoir of insights that inform their responses to challenges. This continuous loop of learning and adaptation fosters resilience, enabling them to face the unpredictable nature of their journey with unwavering confidence.

Ultimately, by embracing reflection as a tool for growth, parents not only enhance their own capabilities but also model a profound lesson for their children. They demonstrate that life's trials are not to be feared but embraced, and that the pursuit of improvement is a noble endeavor. In this way, the growth mindset becomes a shared journey, one that encourages both parent and child to thrive amidst life's uncertainties.

Incorporating Reflection into Daily Life

Incorporating reflection into daily life is not merely an exercise in self-examination; it is an essential practice that nourishes the mind and spirit. The Stoic philosopher understands that life is filled with challenges and triumphs, and it is through reflection that one gains insight into these experiences. Parents, in their vital role, can embrace this practice without the need for elaborate rituals or extensive time commitments.

As the sun sets and the day draws to a close, a few moments of contemplation can reveal much about the trials faced and the victories achieved. It is in these quiet moments that one can ponder the decisions made, the words spoken, and the lessons learned. This does not require extensive analysis but rather a gentle acknowledgment of what transpired. Such reflection serves to illuminate the path forward, fostering a deeper understanding of oneself and one's interactions with others, particularly one's children.

In the stillness of a moment, whether during a morning routine or a brief interlude in the day, parents can take stock of their relationships. How did they respond to their child's needs? What insights can be gleaned from a seemingly ordinary encounter? These reflections do not dwell on regrets but instead focus on growth, transforming each experience into an opportunity for learning.

By embedding reflection into the fabric of daily life, parents cultivate a habit that becomes second nature. This ongoing practice not only grounds them but also enhances their ability to navigate the complexities of parenting with clarity and intention. Each day offers a fresh canvas, and through reflection, they can paint a richer understanding of their journey.

In this way, parenting evolves from a series of tasks into a profound process of continuous learning. Each challenge faced and each success celebrated becomes a stepping stone on the path to wisdom.

The goal is not perfection but progress, fostering resilience and adaptability in both parents and children alike. Through the simple act of reflection, one can embrace the unpredictable nature of life with a stoic heart, remaining focused on what truly matters.

Nine

The Wisdom of Perspective

"Wealth consists not in having great possessions, but in having few wants." – **Epictetus**

The Power of Perspective in Parenting

Stoic Reframing – Turning Challenges into Opportunities
The essence of Stoic philosophy lies in the ability to wield perspective as a tool for resilience. In the realm of parenting, particularly when navigating the complexities of raising children with Sensory Processing Disorder (SPD), this practice becomes paramount. Stoicism reminds us that while we may be at the mercy of external circumstances, our responses to these circumstances are wholly within our control.

When faced with the tumult of sensory overload or emotional upheaval, it is all too easy for parents to succumb to feelings of defeat. Yet, in these moments, Stoicism invites us to adopt a different lens. Instead of perceiving challenges as insurmountable obstacles, we can reframe them as opportunities for growth and learning. For example, when a child experiences an emotional meltdown, instead of viewing it solely as a setback, we can recognize it as a moment rich with potential. It becomes a chance to cultivate patience, to reinforce coping mechanisms, and to model the art of emotional regulation.

This reframing does not diminish the difficulty of the situation; rather, it empowers us to focus on our responses. We acknowledge the chaos inherent in our circumstances while choosing to respond with equanimity. This acceptance of what we cannot control, paired with the commitment to control our reactions, fosters a sense of empowerment. It transforms the narrative from one of struggle to one of resilience and growth.

As we practice this shift in mindset, reframing becomes a habitual response, a cornerstone of our approach to parenting. Each challenge, no matter how formidable, is met with a grounded perspective. We learn to embrace the journey, recognizing that every moment, even the most difficult, holds value and lessons to impart. In this way, we cultivate not only our own emotional resilience but also provide our children with the tools to navigate their own paths with confidence and grace. Thus, we find wealth not in the absence of challenges, but in our ability to desire less in terms of perfection and embrace more in terms of acceptance and understanding.

The Role of Perspective in Emotional Regulation

Perspective serves as a powerful tool in the realm of emotional regulation. It is through the lens we choose to view our circumstances that our emotional experiences are shaped. In the face of challenges, such as those encountered by parents of children with Sensory Processing Disorder (SPD), the ability to adjust one's perspective becomes paramount. When frustration, anxiety, or feelings of helplessness arise, a deliberate shift in viewpoint can transform these negative emotional states into ones characterized by calmness and acceptance.

Consider a scenario where a child's heightened sensory sensitivities lead to distress in a social setting. Instead of perceiving this moment as a crisis demanding immediate rectification, a parent can reframe it as a valuable opportunity for learning and growth. This reframing allows for a more patient and compassionate approach, enabling the parent to embrace the reality that development is a gradual process. Such a perspective encourages resilience, not just in the parent but also in the child.

By modeling this calm and adaptive mindset, parents provide children with an essential framework for managing their own emotional challenges. Children with SPD often find themselves grappling with emotional regulation, and witnessing their parents navigate difficulties with composure teaches them vital lessons. The act of viewing each challenging moment as an opportunity for growth fosters an environment where emotional balance can flourish.

Through this lens, parents become not only custodians of their own emotional well-being but also guides for their children. In cultivating a stable and supportive environment, they reinforce the idea that emotional challenges are not to be feared but embraced as part of the human experience. This perspective, rooted in patience and acceptance, lays the groundwork for resilience, allowing both parents and children to navigate the complexities of their emotions with grace.

Focusing on the Bigger Picture

Parenting a child with Sensory Processing Disorder requires an unwavering commitment to maintaining perspective. In the face of daily sensory challenges, it is easy for emotions to cloud judgment and for the immediate difficulties to seem insurmountable. Yet, the Stoic philosophy teaches us to step back and observe the broader landscape of our lives. By doing so, we can recognize that each moment of struggle is but a fleeting instance in the grand journey of growth and development.

When a sensory episode erupts, the instinctive reaction may be to perceive it as a crisis. However, if we take a moment to reflect, we can see that such episodes are not definitive endpoints but rather integral parts of a much larger narrative. The long-term well-being of the child is not defined by single moments of difficulty but by the continuous progress made over time. Each small victory—whether it be the acquisition of a new coping mechanism or the successful navigation of a challenging situation—should be celebrated, for these are the building blocks of resilience.

In embracing this broader perspective, a parent cultivates patience. They understand that growth is not linear and that the path is often fraught with obstacles. This insight fosters resilience, as challenges become opportunities for learning rather than sources of despair. By focusing on the long-term goals and the incremental advancements made, parents can maintain a sense of hope and purpose.

This stoic approach is not merely about enduring difficulties but about finding meaning within them. It is a commitment to view parenting as a journey of mutual growth, where both parent and child learn and evolve together. In the face of adversity, the stoic parent remains grounded, drawing strength from the knowledge that the struggles faced today will contribute to the strength and character of tomorrow. Thus, by focusing on the bigger picture, they nurture a deeper connection with their child, fostering an environment where both can thrive amidst challenges.

"Resilience is the ability to attack while running away." – Walter Inglis Anderso

Shifting Perspective to Foster Resilience in Children with SPD

Teaching Children to Reframe Their Experiences

Teaching children to reframe their experiences is essential in fostering resilience, particularly for those grappling with Sensory Processing Disorder (SPD). The ability to shift one's perspective can transform adversity into a source of strength. Children who encounter sensory overload or social challenges often find themselves ensnared in feelings of frustration and helplessness. It is within the power of their guardians to guide them towards a more constructive mindset.

When confronted with discomfort, such as the overwhelming sounds of a bustling environment, it is vital for children to learn the practice of reframing. Instead of fixating on the chaos surrounding them, parents can encourage their children to consider the strategies at their disposal. For instance, the use of noise-canceling headphones or seeking refuge in a quieter space can be framed as tools for empowerment rather than mere escapes from discomfort. This subtle shift in focus not only diminishes anxiety but also instills a sense of agency in the child, allowing them to navigate their sensory sensitivities with intention and purpose.

Encouraging children to view sensory challenges as opportunities for growth is crucial in this process. Each encounter with discomfort can serve as a training ground for developing coping skills. Rather than viewing these moments as setbacks, children can be taught to embrace them as chances to cultivate resilience. This perspective fosters a growth mindset, wherein the child learns that their abilities can be developed through effort and practice.

As children adopt a more positive and growth-oriented perspective, they gradually build confidence in their ability to face sensory experiences. This confidence is key in reducing fear and anxiety. Over time, the consistent practice of reframing experiences contributes to the development of emotional intelligence and self-regulation. These skills are indispensable for effectively managing SPD and navigating the complexities of the world.

In essence, the act of reframing is not merely a coping strategy; it is a pathway to resilience. By instilling this practice in children, parents equip them with the tools necessary to approach life's challenges with a sense of empowerment and adaptability. In doing so, they prepare their children not only to manage their sensory sensitivities but also to thrive amidst the uncertainties of life.

Using Gratitude as a Tool for Perspective

Gratitude serves as a formidable tool for cultivating perspective, particularly in the face of adversity. In moments of overwhelm or frustration, children with Sensory Processing Disorder (SPD) may find themselves ensnared by their circumstances. Yet, by embracing gratitude, they can redirect their focus toward the positive elements that persist even in challenging times.

Parents play a crucial role in this practice, guiding their children to identify and articulate the aspects of their lives for which they are thankful. This process may involve recognizing their own resilience in dealing with sensory overload, appreciating the unwavering support of their family, or celebrating the smaller victories that often go unnoticed amidst turmoil. By shifting the lens through which they view their experiences, children learn to acknowledge what is working in their favor rather than fixating on the difficulties they face.

For instance, during a sensory overload episode, rather than succumbing to despair, a child can reflect on the strategies they employed to regain composure—such as taking deliberate deep breaths or utilizing a fidget toy for self-soothing. This reflection not only highlights their capacity to manage the situation but also reinforces the notion that challenges, while daunting, are not insurmountable.

In this practice of gratitude, children cultivate emotional resilience, empowering them to confront future difficulties with a mindset rooted in strength and appreciation. The act of recognizing their capabilities fosters a deeper understanding that life's trials are opportunities for growth rather than mere obstacles. Through the lens of gratitude, they learn to navigate their experiences with a renewed sense of purpose and a belief in their inherent ability to overcome.

Modeling Perspective Shifts as Parents

Parents serve as the foremost exemplars in their children's lives, shaping their understanding of the world and their place within it. In their responses to life's inevitable challenges, parents impart lessons that extend far beyond words. When they confront adversity with a mindset grounded in positivity and adaptability, they lay the foundation for their children to embrace similar virtues. This modeling of perspective shifts during moments of stress or overwhelm becomes a profound gift, equipping children with the skills necessary to navigate their own trials.

Consider a scenario where a parent experiences sensory overload while in a crowded space. Instead of succumbing to the chaos, they can demonstrate a composed assessment of the situation, thoughtfully reframing their perspective to seek clarity amidst the noise.

This act of reflection and adjustment not only calms the moment but also serves as a powerful lesson for children, particularly those grappling with sensory processing difficulties. Such children often find themselves adrift in emotional turmoil, overwhelmed by experiences that others may navigate with ease. When parents illustrate that challenges can be perceived as opportunities for growth, they instill a sense of resilience that fortifies their children against the storms of life.

These lessons, practiced consistently, become ingrained in the psyche of both parent and child. Over time, they foster a shared journey marked by peace and understanding. As parents embody the stoic principles of acceptance and adaptability, they cultivate an environment where children can thrive, learning to face their own sensory challenges with confidence and calmness. In this way, the act of modeling perspective shifts transcends mere behavior; it becomes a pathway to emotional strength, guiding both generations toward a more harmonious existence in the face of life's trials.

Perspective Shifts for Personal Growth and Empowerment

Reframing Parenting as a Journey of Growth

Reframing parenting as a journey of growth encourages a profound understanding of the trials faced by those raising a child with Sensory Processing Disorder (SPD). The Stoic philosophy reminds us that challenges are not mere obstacles but rather essential components of our development. Each struggle serves as a crucible in which our virtues are tested and fortified.

To approach parenting through this lens is to embrace the notion that every difficulty provides a chance for self-reflection and enhancement of character. When parents encounter the fatigue and frustration inherent in managing SPD, they can consciously choose to see these moments not as burdens but as invitations to cultivate patience, resilience, and emotional intelligence. In doing so, they align themselves with the Stoic ideal of transforming adversity into strength.

Consider a particularly arduous day, marked by overwhelming sensory sensitivities and emotional turmoil. A parent might initially perceive this as a failure, a moment of inadequacy in their role. However, through the Stoic practice of reframing, they can recognize this day as a valuable opportunity. It becomes a canvas for practicing the very virtues they seek to embody—patience in the face of chaos, resilience when confronted with repeated setbacks, and emotional intelligence as they navigate their child's needs.

This shift in perspective fosters a sense of empowerment, as parents understand that their journey is not solely about the child's development but also their own. Each challenge faced is a step towards becoming a more capable and compassionate individual. By acknowledging the potential for growth within these trials, parents can cultivate a mindset that embraces difficulty as a vital part of their evolution.

In essence, the Stoic approach to parenting reframes hardship as a teacher, enabling parents to walk their path with a sense of purpose. In this way, they transform their experiences into lessons, enriching their lives with greater understanding and deeper connections. Each challenge met with a spirit of growth not only empowers the parent but also enriches the environment in which the child learns and thrives.

Carl Rogers – Embracing Empathy and Reflection on the Journey

Carl Rogers' contributions to humanistic psychology and the development of client-centered therapy have left a lasting mark on how we understand personal growth. Rogers believed that true growth and self-actualization could only emerge when individuals felt truly understood, accepted, and supported—an environment where judgment is absent, and empathy reigns. Central to his philosophy is the concept of *unconditional positive regard*, a practice where we accept others for who they are, regardless of their behaviors or feelings, without trying to change or fix them.

For parents raising children with Sensory Processing Disorder (SPD), Rogers' philosophy couldn't be more relevant. SPD presents challenges that are often invisible to others. The way children react to sensory stimuli—loud sounds, bright lights, crowded spaces—can leave parents feeling confused or frustrated. This is where the power of empathy comes in. Just as Rogers taught us to truly listen and understand a person's experience, parents must invest time in genuinely understanding their child's sensory world. Instead of rushing to fix or change the behavior, we shift our perspective from frustration to insight, allowing us to see our child's experience through their eyes. In this understanding, we find the keys to connection and effective support.

Rogers taught us to approach each situation from the other person's point of view, rather than imposing our own judgments. For parents, this means recognizing that a child's sensory challenges are not problems to be solved but part of their unique way of interacting with the world. When parents respond with empathy instead of trying to correct behavior, they foster a deeper, more meaningful connection with their child. This shift—from external judgment to internal understanding—nurtures resilience for both the child and the parent. It creates an environment where both can grow, learn, and thrive.

One of Rogers' key teachings was the importance of self-reflection, and it's something parents can greatly benefit from. When we pause to reflect on our responses to sensory overloads, emotional outbursts, or challenging moments, we shift our perspective. Instead of seeing our child's reactions as personal affronts, we recognize them for what they truly are: expressions of sensory processing difficulties. By practicing non-judgmental reflection, we gain clarity and patience, helping us respond with compassion rather than frustration.

Rogers put it beautifully when he said, *"The curious paradox is that when I accept myself just as I am, then I can change."* This captures the essence of his philosophy—true transformation begins with acceptance. For parents, accepting our child's sensory needs and emotional responses, just as they are, without trying to force change, is the first step toward fostering growth. By embracing acceptance, we create a nurturing space for both the child and ourselves to flourish.

Carl Rogers' insights remind us that change doesn't come from forcing transformation—it comes from shifting our perspective and adopting a stance of empathy and non-judgment. In doing so, we open ourselves up to a world of deeper understanding and connection. Just as Rogers saw empathy and reflection as tools for growth, parents of children with SPD can use these principles to navigate challenges, turning each one into an opportunity for stronger bonds and personal growth. In embracing this journey, we can create a space for our children to thrive, and in doing so, transform ourselves as well.

Using Perspective to Build Empathy and Compassion

The practice of shifting our perspective is a powerful tool in cultivating empathy and compassion. When we adopt a mindset that views challenges as opportunities for growth, we inherently become more patient and understanding, not only towards ourselves but also towards others. For parents navigating the complexities of raising children with Sensory Processing Disorder, this perspective is particularly vital.

Empathy allows parents to engage with their child's experiences on a deeper level. By reframing moments of struggle as chances for connection, they can approach their child's sensory difficulties with a heart full of compassion. Recognizing that these sensitivities are integral to their child's identity rather than something that requires fixing is a profound realization. It shifts the narrative from one of frustration to one of acceptance, creating a space where understanding can flourish.

This enhanced empathy not only aids in supporting the child but also ripples through the family dynamic. When parents embody compassion, it fosters an atmosphere of mutual understanding among all family members. Each individual can see the challenges faced and respond with kindness rather than judgment. This interconnectedness strengthens familial bonds, allowing everyone to feel heard and valued.

In cultivating such a perspective, parents can guide their children through their unique experiences with grace. They are equipped to offer support that acknowledges and honors their child's needs, leading to a more harmonious household. Through empathy, families can turn the trials of life into a shared journey of growth, learning, and deeper connection. In doing so, they not only enrich their own lives but also create an environment where every member can thrive authentically.

Empowering Ourselves Through Perspective

Perspective in our world is everything. Take, for instance, a situation where one person sees an impending conflict, while another hears a chance for peace talks. For me, a disagreement could feel like it's heading toward violence, while someone else might view it as a simple misunderstanding, ready for resolution. Now, not everything needs to be that dramatic, of course, but perspective is key. It shapes how we interpret the world and how we approach challenges, both big and small.

If we only take the negatives from a situation, if we focus solely on what went wrong, there will inevitably be a shift in how we view things that aren't inherently negative. This leads to a skewed outlook, where even neutral or positive situations are viewed through a pessimistic lens. I've seen this pattern in my own journey. In a situation where I might have only succeeded in 2 out of 10 attempts, it's easy to focus on the 8 that didn't work out. But by doing that, I miss the fact that, despite the failures, I proved that it can work. And that's where the shift in perspective needs to happen. It's not about focusing on the failures; it's about reinforcing the successes and using them as a foundation to build on.

Consider the next 10 attempts. If, over time, I start succeeding 4 out of 10 times instead of just 2, that's progress. It's growth. And from there, it can only continue to improve. But the key is not giving up after the first, second, or tenth failure. The problem with focusing only on the negative is that it leads us to quit before we've given ourselves the chance to succeed. We stop short of the improvement we seek simply because we've failed to shift our perspective.

Our perspective doesn't just shape how we see the world; it also profoundly impacts how our children will see the world. If we constantly show them that giving up is acceptable, that failure is final, they will internalize that mindset as they grow. It creates a negative pattern that becomes difficult to break. Imagine if, every time my son struggles with something, I just accept that it's too hard and that he should move on. What would that teach him? That success is only for those who never fail, which we all know is simply untrue.

"Success is not in avoiding failure; it's in learning to fail forward, growing stronger with each step, and embracing the journey as a whole." – **The Philosophical Dad**

The story of *Jason and the Argonauts* serves as a powerful example of how perspective shapes our journey, especially when facing challenges. Jason, tasked with retrieving the Golden Fleece, embarks on a perilous journey filled with trials that test both his physical and mental strength. Along the way, Jason encounters fierce monsters, treacherous seas, and even betrayal by those closest to him. But rather than letting these obstacles deter him, Jason shifts his perspective. He adapts, learns from each setback, and uses the strengths of his allies to overcome every hurdle. Each failure, each trial, becomes a lesson—a stepping stone toward his ultimate goal.

Much like Jason, we must approach challenges not with defeat in mind but with the understanding that each failure is a chance to refine our methods. Jason's journey teaches us that it's not the challenges that define us but how we respond to them. He didn't allow setbacks to dictate his fate; instead, he embraced each challenge as an opportunity for growth and resilience. This mindset is essential for both us and our children—teaching them that failure is not a dead end, but a part of the journey that can be learned from and overcome with patience, adaptability, and persistence.

Empowering ourselves through perspective is an essential practice in the art of living, particularly in the realm of parenting a child with sensory processing disorder. The journey is laden with complexities, yet it is within our grasp to navigate these challenges with a stoic mindset. By anchoring our focus on what lies within our control—our actions, our reactions, and our mindset—we cultivate a clarity that illuminates the path forward.

The challenges we face may seem daunting, but they are not insurmountable. Each obstacle can be perceived as a stepping stone for personal growth, a chance to learn more about ourselves and our capacities. In this reframing, we discover that our emotional resilience is fortified through adversity. We recognize that while we cannot dictate the sensory experiences our child endures, we possess the power to shape our response. Our emotional state, our patience, and our understanding are all within our dominion.

This shift in perspective allows us to approach our role with renewed vigor and purpose. The act of embracing challenges transforms them into opportunities for development—not only for our children but for ourselves as well. In acknowledging the significance of our growth, we find motivation and inspiration that propels us forward. The journey of parenting is not solely about the child's progress; it is equally about our evolution as individuals.

In this light, we cultivate a sense of purpose that informs our daily actions. Embracing the responsibility of parenting becomes a noble endeavor, a chance to exemplify resilience and adaptability. Each moment spent navigating the intricacies of sensory experiences can serve as a profound lesson, teaching us patience and empathy. Through this lens, we understand that our struggles are not merely burdens but rather catalysts for profound personal development.

Thus, we step into the role of the empowered parent, recognizing that our perspective is a powerful tool. It shapes our reality, influences our emotional state, and ultimately defines our journey. By consciously choosing to focus on the constructive aspects of our experiences, we find strength in vulnerability and wisdom in uncertainty. In this way, we not only support our child in their journey but also honor our own path of growth and resilience.

Ten

Embracing Patience

"**W**e *are what we repeatedly do. Excellence, then, is not an act, but a habit.*" – **Aristotle**

The Stoic concept that virtue and excellence are not merely single acts but the result of repeated actions that cultivate good habits. In Stoicism, the focus is not on fleeting moments of greatness but on consistently choosing virtuous actions, no matter how small. This idea resonates deeply with the Stoic path, where we are encouraged to work toward inner tranquility and emotional mastery through habitual practice. Stoicism teaches us that our character is forged not through grand gestures but through our day-to-day choices. The accumulation of positive choices, even when they seem insignificant in the moment, defines who we are and shapes our future.

In the context of SPD, this Stoic principle becomes incredibly powerful. Parenting a child with sensory processing disorder requires ongoing patience, emotional regulation, and understanding—virtues that need to be practiced consistently. Just like Aristotle suggests, excellence in parenting doesn't come from a single heroic act but from the habit of showing up, time and time again, with a calm, steady, and empathetic approach. It's about creating a daily routine of responses that align with Stoic principles, regardless of the challenges faced. This process allows us to grow into more virtuous parents, cultivating habits that enable us to handle adversity with grace.

When we apply it to Sensory Processing Disorder, it speaks directly to the necessity of consistency in managing sensory sensitivities. Sensory overloads and emotional meltdowns are not isolated incidents—they are recurring patterns. Parents of children with SPD often face the same struggles over and over again: loud noises, bright lights, or overwhelming environments. To manage these challenges effectively, parents must develop a deep well of patience and adaptability, which only grows through consistent practice. It's easy to get frustrated, especially when it feels like progress is slow, but embracing the idea that excellence is a habit encourages us to persevere and continue refining our responses. Over time, these habitual responses, grounded in Stoic virtues, become second nature.

For a child with SPD, experiencing consistent, positive responses from their parents provides them with a stable foundation. Children thrive on consistency, and when parents model patience, understanding, and emotional regulation, they teach their children how to manage their sensory experiences with the same virtues. Just as a Stoic would approach their daily struggles with self-discipline and understanding, a child with SPD can learn to navigate their challenges in a calm, measured way. The repeated, steady practice of responding with calmness in overwhelming situations eventually teaches the child that they can rely on their emotional regulation techniques to soothe themselves, reinforcing resilience and self-confidence over time.

Aristotle's idea that "excellence is a habit" invites parents to reflect on their own actions and reactions. How do we consistently show up for our children? The challenges that come with SPD can feel exhausting, but the habits we cultivate as parents will set the tone for the entire family. By being mindful of our responses and making a conscious effort to choose patience, empathy, and understanding, we can improve our interactions with our child. These small, daily actions compound over time, creating an environment of consistency and stability where both parent and child can thrive. As we practice these virtues daily, we begin to see the transformation not only in ourselves but in our child as well. Just as Stoicism teaches us to focus on what we can control, the act of consistently showing up with presence and virtue gives us the tools to navigate even the most challenging moments.

This principle also invites us to evaluate how we respond to the inevitable setbacks along the way. When a parent feels discouraged by a particularly tough moment or the repetition of sensory challenges, it's easy to fall into frustration. However, recognizing that *excellence* is built from these very repetitions—the practice of *starting again* with patience and understanding—is what leads to lasting progress. It's not about perfection in the moment; it's about growth through consistent effort. By embracing this mindset, both parents and children can progress in their understanding of SPD, becoming better equipped to deal with challenges in a more positive, empowered way.

Raising a child with SPD, Aristotle's wisdom resonates as a reminder that true excellence in parenting is a continual process, rooted in consistent habits. It encourages us as parents to engage with our children, not in rare moments of brilliance, but in everyday, ordinary ways. It's the repeated practice of patience, understanding, and emotional regulation that ultimately leads to profound transformation—both for ourselves as parents and for our children as they learn to manage their sensory sensitivities. Through consistent application of these virtues, we can cultivate a home environment where growth, resilience, and understanding flourish.

As a virtue and a way of assessing my life and being situationally aware of what's happening around me, patience is one of my favorite virtues. It allows for clear and concise communication, especially when things aren't going as expected. It provides room for de-escalation, where the intensity of the moment can be softened, and it opens the door for personal reflection. Patience, in its purest form, offers us the chance to pause, collect ourselves, and respond in a measured, thoughtful manner. But as with any virtue, patience on its own can feel incomplete. It needs to be accompanied by the other Stoic virtues to truly be effective.

For example, patience needs to be met with wisdom. What is patience if you don't know how to apply it effectively? Without wisdom, patience can easily be misguided or misused, leading us to tolerate situations that should be addressed. Similarly, justice must also be a part of the equation. Just because a child has sensory issues doesn't mean they get a free pass. Actions have consequences, and as parents, we must approach our children's behavior with fairness and consistency. However, this justice needs to be tempered with patience and wisdom. For instance, if a child acts out, it's important to calmly assess whether they are overwhelmed by sensory overload or if they are simply testing boundaries. Applying wisdom here ensures that we don't react too harshly but also don't let behavior slide when consequences are necessary.

The fourth virtue, courage, also plays a critical role in balancing patience. Courage is necessary when we need to step in and set boundaries, even when it's uncomfortable. It takes courage to be patient in the face of your child's challenging behavior, especially when you're emotionally drained, and to maintain the self-control required to guide them through their emotions. The virtues work together—patience allows us to pause, wisdom helps us to understand, justice ensures fairness, and courage gives us the strength to take the right action when needed.

Patience, when combined with the other virtues, allows us as parents to step back from the heat of the moment and carefully examine what our child needs. Does the child require removal from a situation to calm down? Do we need to remove others from the situation to give our child space? Are our own reactions contributing to the escalation? Patience provides us with the clarity to discern the best course of action. It's an incredibly powerful tool, but it requires practice. When we know when and how to use patience, it transforms not only how we parent but also how we handle life's challenges.

"Patience is not just about waiting. It's about creating space to reflect, allowing us to see the bigger picture, so that our decisions can lead to growth rather than regret." – **The Philosophical Dad**

This idea of patience and its relation to decision-making mirrors the story of *The Golden Apple and the Trojan War*. In this myth, Paris, the prince of Troy, is given a golden apple by the goddess Eris, which she claims should be awarded to the fairest goddess. Paris, faced with the decision of which goddess deserves the apple—Hera, Athena, or Aphrodite—rushes into making his choice without fully considering the consequences. Each goddess offers Paris a tempting reward, and Paris, drawn to Aphrodite's promise of the most beautiful woman in the world, chooses her. His decision, made without patience or full reflection, ultimately leads to the Trojan War.

Much like Paris, when we rush through decisions or fail to reflect on the consequences, we often end up facing the unintended results of our actions. If Paris had taken the time to weigh the impact of his choice, he might have avoided the catastrophic war that followed. In parenting, we often face moments where a hasty decision could lead to regret. It's in those times that patience—pausing to consider our child's needs, our own emotions, and the long-term consequences of our actions—becomes invaluable. When we slow down, reflect, and make thoughtful decisions, we steer clear of unnecessary conflict and allow growth to take place.

The myth of Paris and the Golden Apple is a reminder that impatience in decision-making can lead to lasting consequences, both for ourselves and our children. By practicing patience, we give ourselves the space to think, reflect, and choose the most thoughtful course of action—one that not only resolves the current issue but fosters understanding and growth for the future. Like Paris, we may face choices every day that can shift the course of our relationships and our lives, but it is our ability to pause, reflect, and act with patience that shapes the outcomes.

Cultivating Virtue in Parenting

When raising a child with Sensory Processing Disorder (SPD), it's easy to feel overwhelmed by the daily challenges that arise. However, the Stoic virtues of wisdom, courage, justice, and temperance offer powerful tools for navigating these difficulties and creating a strong, stable foundation for both parents and children. By applying these virtues consistently, parents can build an environment where their child not only learns to manage their sensory sensitivities but also thrives emotionally and socially. Let's explore how each of these virtues can be woven into the fabric of everyday parenting, particularly in the context of SPD.

Wisdom, the first of the Stoic virtues, plays a crucial role in understanding and navigating the sensory needs of a child with SPD.

Wisdom allows parents to identify the underlying causes of sensory overload and recognize patterns in their child's reactions. Instead of reacting impulsively or with frustration, parents can use their wisdom to assess the situation calmly, making thoughtful decisions based on their knowledge of the child's specific sensory triggers. This requires active listening, keen observation, and ongoing learning about SPD. When parents take the time to understand their child's unique sensory experiences, they are better equipped to respond in a way that supports and nurtures the child, rather than escalating the situation.

Courage is the virtue that empowers parents to face the many unknowns that come with raising a child with SPD. It takes courage to stay patient and calm when your child is overwhelmed by sensory inputs that others may not notice. It also takes courage to advocate for your child in social situations or educational environments where people may not fully understand or accommodate their needs. Courage allows parents to face these challenges head-on, without allowing fear or self-doubt to take over. By embodying courage, parents not only help their children cope with their sensory sensitivities but also model resilience and bravery in the face of adversity, teaching their children that it's okay to confront difficult situations with strength and dignity.

Justice as a Stoic virtue involves fairness, respect, and the recognition of the rights of others. When parenting a child with SPD, justice means advocating for their needs and ensuring they have the resources and support they require. It means being fair in your expectations, setting boundaries that are not punitive but instead supportive of the child's emotional and sensory regulation. Justice also extends to the way a parent treats themselves. Parents of children with SPD often experience burnout, and practicing justice means being fair to oneself by recognizing the need for rest and self-care.

By cultivating justice, parents can create a balanced and supportive environment where the child's needs are met, and where fairness, respect, and mutual understanding are central to the family dynamic.

Finally, **Temperance** is the virtue that helps parents manage their emotional responses, especially in times of stress or sensory overload. Children with SPD often have intense reactions to seemingly minor stimuli, and as a parent, it's easy to become frustrated or anxious when these reactions occur. Temperance allows parents to pause before reacting, taking a moment to reflect and respond with understanding rather than emotion. It teaches parents to find balance, not only in their interactions with their children but also in their approach to handling the challenges that come with SPD. By practicing temperance, parents can remain grounded, ensuring that their responses are measured and thoughtful, which in turn fosters a calmer, more stable environment for the child.

When these four Stoic virtues—wisdom, courage, justice, and temperance—are implemented in the context of parenting a child with SPD, they create a strong framework for emotional and behavioral growth. These virtues allow parents to build a supportive, empathetic, and resilient approach to their child's unique challenges. By consistently practicing these virtues, parents can not only help their children navigate the difficulties of SPD but also foster their own growth, learning, and emotional well-being. With patience, persistence, and a commitment to living by these values, the parent-child relationship can flourish, providing a foundation of stability and love that supports the child through all of life's sensory and emotional challenges.

Parenting with a Stoic Mindset

When we think about Stoic parenting, it's not about applying rigid rules but about shifting the mindset. A parent with a Stoic mindset approaches parenting with purpose and clarity, choosing to respond to challenges with equanimity rather than frustration. When raising a child with SPD, sensory overload or emotional meltdowns are frequent, and how a parent chooses to respond in these moments can either escalate or de-escalate the situation. A Stoic parent remains calm, centered, and focused on long-term solutions, not immediate emotional reactions. This mindset cultivates a steady foundation, teaching children that their emotional responses can be managed, even when overwhelmed.

For example, emotional regulation becomes a key aspect of Stoic parenting. When a child becomes distressed by sensory stimuli, the parent, instead of reacting impulsively, chooses to respond with patience and understanding. The focus isn't on fixing the child's behavior but on managing the situation in a way that offers comfort and safety. This approach allows the child to feel heard and supported, which reinforces trust and helps them feel secure in their environment. Stoicism teaches us that while we cannot control external events, we can control how we respond to them, and this mindset is essential when navigating the unpredictability of SPD.

Through this lens, wisdom comes into play: the ability to recognize patterns in the child's sensory experiences and act with thoughtful consideration. Instead of seeing challenges as problems to be fixed, a Stoic parent views them as opportunities for growth—both for themselves and for their child. This change in perspective fosters resilience and long-term emotional well-being for the child.

Incorporating Stoic principles into parenting is an ongoing practice, not a one-time fix. It involves staying present and mindful in each interaction, recognizing that each moment is an opportunity to guide the child toward emotional growth. By doing so, parents cultivate a sense of purpose in their approach, creating a stable foundation for both themselves and their child.

The Balance of Understanding and Action

Understanding a child's sensory needs is one thing, but action is required to create real change. Parenting a child with SPD requires a delicate balance: parents must understand the sensory overload that their child experiences, but they must also take practical steps to manage it. The Stoic virtue of wisdom plays an important role here, as parents use their understanding of SPD to decide on the best course of action. Whether it's removing the child from a stressful environment, using calming techniques, or offering sensory tools, taking thoughtful action becomes part of the process of helping the child navigate their sensory world.

At the same time, the virtue of courage supports parents in facing the unknowns of SPD. It takes courage to step out of your comfort zone, especially when the usual strategies don't seem to work. Courage also plays a role when advocating for your child's needs in various settings, from school to social situations, where others may not fully understand the complexities of SPD. By embodying courage, parents become the child's advocates, ensuring that their needs are met in ways that promote their well-being and emotional regulation.

However, understanding and action alone are not enough without justice—the fairness to provide accommodations for the child and set clear, realistic expectations. Justice ensures that the child is treated equitably, acknowledging their sensory challenges without letting them become a reason for disregarding appropriate expectations and boundaries. Parents learn to set reasonable limits while ensuring that their child's sensory sensitivities are always considered.

By balancing these aspects—understanding, action, courage, and justice—parents can help their children thrive in the face of sensory challenges. This approach ensures that both the child's needs and the family's well-being are respected and nurtured, creating a positive and sustainable approach to managing SPD.

Consistency and Adaptability in Parenting Strategies

When it comes to raising a child with SPD, consistency is a key ingredient for success. Children with SPD often feel more secure when they know what to expect, especially in moments of sensory overload. Consistent responses help the child feel stable, even in the midst of chaos. However, while consistency is vital, adaptability is equally important. The child's sensory needs can evolve over time, and what works one day may not work the next. This requires a level of flexibility and a willingness to reassess strategies regularly.

The Stoic virtue of temperance is central to maintaining both consistency and adaptability. Parents need to practice emotional regulation and patience when things don't go according to plan. It can be frustrating when the strategies that worked yesterday no longer seem effective today. Temperance teaches parents to take a step back and not react in frustration, but rather to assess the situation calmly and make necessary adjustments. By remaining balanced in their approach, parents can adjust their responses while still maintaining the consistency the child needs to feel safe.

Wisdom is crucial here as well. By being attuned to their child's emotional state, parents can recognize when a situation requires a shift in strategy. This wisdom doesn't come from sticking rigidly to one method but from understanding what the child truly needs in the moment. For example, if a child is particularly sensitive to noise, a quiet space might be more beneficial than a sensory tool. Understanding that one size doesn't fit all is key in adapting strategies to meet the child's evolving needs.

Ultimately, the ability to adapt while staying consistent in core principles allows parents to be more responsive to their child's changing sensory needs. This approach builds a sense of trust between parent and child, ensuring the child feels supported and safe even as their needs shift.

The Role of Reflection in Long-Term Growth

Reflection is a powerful tool in Stoic parenting. It allows parents to review their actions, understand how their responses impact their child, and adjust strategies for the future. For parents of children with SPD, reflection is especially important because sensory challenges often lead to high-stress moments that can cloud judgment. Taking time at the end of the day to reflect on the experiences, evaluate the emotional responses, and think about what worked—and what didn't—provides valuable insight into both the child's development and the parent's growth.

Incorporating wisdom and temperance into this reflection is key. Wisdom helps parents understand their emotional reactions and learn from past experiences. For example, if a parent notices that they reacted with frustration during a sensory meltdown, they can reflect on what caused that response and make adjustments for the future. Temperance allows them to approach these reflections with a calm and clear mindset, free from self-judgment or guilt, focusing on improvement rather than perfection.

Reflection also enables parents to celebrate progress, no matter how small. When a strategy works well, it's important to acknowledge and appreciate the improvement, reinforcing the child's growth and the parent's ability to adapt. This helps build confidence in both the child and the parent, encouraging further progress in managing SPD.

By regularly engaging in reflective practice, parents can enhance their ability to parent effectively, develop more effective strategies for their child, and deepen the parent-child bond. Reflection allows parents to stay focused on the long-term goal of raising a resilient, emotionally regulated child and provides a space to acknowledge the small wins that add up to meaningful change over time.

Embracing the Journey of Parenting with Virtue

Parenting a child with SPD is a long, often unpredictable journey. It's easy to become focused on the end goal: a child who can manage their sensory sensitivities with ease. However, the Stoic mindset teaches us to embrace the journey itself—the small moments of progress, the setbacks, and the opportunities for growth. By practicing Stoic virtues every day, parents can view each challenge as an opportunity to cultivate patience, wisdom, and resilience.

Instead of focusing solely on achieving a particular outcome, Stoic parenting encourages parents to embrace the process. This approach is especially important when dealing with SPD, where progress might be slow and uneven. Embracing the journey means being patient with both the child and yourself, recognizing that growth takes time, and trusting that each step, no matter how small, contributes to long-term success.

By practicing virtue, parents can learn to navigate the emotional ups and downs of the journey with a sense of calm and purpose.

Each challenge becomes a chance to strengthen the family's bond and grow in emotional intelligence. This mindset not only helps parents manage their child's SPD but also empowers them to become better, more resilient individuals.

Instilling Self-Discipline and Responsibility

The Importance of Self-Discipline in Children with SPD

When it comes to parenting children with SPD, one of the most important aspects of their development is self-discipline. Children with sensory sensitivities often struggle with emotional regulation, and part of helping them navigate their world is teaching them how to manage their own responses. This is where the Stoic virtues become invaluable. By practicing temperance, parents can model how to manage their emotions in the face of overwhelming stimuli. Just as wisdom helps parents recognize the need for self-regulation, courage enables them to consistently respond to their child's emotional challenges with calmness and understanding.

Self-discipline doesn't come easily for children with SPD, especially when they can't always control how they react to sensory stimuli. However, teaching them self-discipline is essential for their emotional growth and well-being. For example, a child may become upset by loud noises or bright lights, but with consistent support and guidance, they can learn to implement strategies like deep breathing or seeking a quiet space to regain control. This process of teaching self-discipline may take time and patience, but the long-term benefits—both for the child and the parent—are significant. When a child with SPD starts to recognize the importance of emotional regulation, it empowers them to take control of their responses in increasingly difficult situations.

The Stoic mindset is incredibly helpful in guiding parents toward a healthy approach to teaching self-discipline. The understanding that we cannot control external events, but we can control our responses to them, aligns perfectly with helping children with SPD regulate their emotions. Parents must consistently model self-discipline through their own behavior, practicing emotional regulation, taking responsibility for their reactions, and maintaining a sense of calm control, even when things seem chaotic.

Creating Routines to Build Responsibility

A consistent routine can work wonders for children with SPD. Children often feel more secure and less anxious when they know what to expect. A predictable routine creates a sense of control in an often unpredictable world, which is incredibly important for children dealing with sensory sensitivities. Stoicism teaches us the importance of self-control in the face of challenges, and creating a routine that provides structure and support is a way to teach children how to handle the unknown with confidence. The more predictable the routine, the less overwhelming the day will feel for a child with SPD, which provides them with the mental space to regulate their sensory needs.

Routines also promote a sense of responsibility in children. When they know what is expected of them and what comes next, they feel more in control of their own actions. For example, when a child consistently follows a morning routine—brushing their teeth, getting dressed, and preparing for the day—they start to feel a sense of accomplishment and responsibility. The virtue of justice comes into play here, as parents ensure their child has clear expectations and consequences, creating a balance between nurturing independence and maintaining appropriate boundaries. Parents should also consider including sensory breaks or calming activities in the routine to help the child manage sensory overload throughout the day.

The virtue of wisdom is critical in designing a routine that is flexible enough to accommodate the child's sensory needs while still teaching responsibility. Parents may find that the routine needs to be adjusted over time, and wisdom allows them to assess what is working and what isn't. Over time, the child learns that self-discipline and responsibility are important, and they start internalizing those behaviors, making them a part of their everyday routine.

The Role of Consequences and Accountability

For a child with SPD, understanding that their actions have consequences is essential for emotional growth. The Stoic principle of justice comes into play here, as it ensures that children are held accountable for their behavior while still being treated with compassion and understanding. While it's important to acknowledge the challenges that come with SPD, it's equally important for children to learn that their actions—whether positive or negative—have an impact on those around them.

A child who is consistently given clear consequences for their behavior, both good and bad, starts to understand the relationship between their actions and the outcomes. For example, if a child has a sensory meltdown and responds inappropriately to others, there must be a consequence that is related to the behavior, such as a short time-out or a break from the situation. However, the key is to pair this with empathy—acknowledging that the child is struggling with sensory overload, not intentionally misbehaving. Through this balanced approach of accountability and compassion, children learn to take responsibility for their actions while feeling supported through their sensory struggles.

The virtue of courage is necessary for parents when enforcing consequences. It can be difficult to impose consequences in stressful moments, especially when the child is overwhelmed. But courage allows parents to act with clarity, consistency, and fairness. By maintaining a steady, calm approach, parents demonstrate that responsibility is important even when emotions are high. The goal isn't to punish the child but to teach them that their actions are connected to the world around them and that they can make choices that lead to better outcomes.

Modeling Self-Discipline Through Parental Actions

One of the most effective ways to teach self-discipline is through modeling. Children, especially those with SPD, are highly observant of their parents' behaviors. If parents consistently demonstrate self-discipline in their own actions, it sends a powerful message to the child. This means emotionally regulating responses to stressors, delaying gratification, and prioritizing long-term goals over short-term desires. For example, when a parent faces a difficult situation—whether it's a sensory overload moment or a challenging social event—they can model self-discipline by staying calm and thoughtful in their responses.

The virtue of temperance plays a central role in this process. When parents model emotional regulation and patience in high-stress situations, they provide a living example of how to navigate challenges with composure. Children with SPD are often in situations where their sensory sensitivities can lead to emotional outbursts. When they see their parents handle similar stress with calmness and rational thinking, they learn how to manage their emotions in similar situations.

It's also important for parents to model self-discipline in their daily habits. Whether it's maintaining a consistent routine, exercising self-control with technology, or practicing mindfulness, children are always watching and absorbing these behaviors. By demonstrating how to stay focused, stay calm, and approach challenges with patience, parents teach their children how to do the same.

Through consistent modeling of self-discipline, parents not only help their child develop their own sense of responsibility but also create a safe, predictable environment where the child can feel supported while learning how to regulate their sensory experiences.

Balancing Compassion and Accountability

Balancing compassion and accountability is one of the most important aspects of parenting a child with SPD. It's easy to fall into the trap of being overly lenient because the child is struggling with sensory sensitivities, but justice requires that parents also hold the child accountable for their actions. The Stoic approach to justice is about fairness and balance—it's about ensuring that children understand the consequences of their actions, but in a way that is empathetic and supportive.

Compassion plays a significant role when managing SPD because children often don't have control over their sensory experiences. They may become distressed or overwhelmed, but that doesn't mean their behavior should go unchecked. Compassion involves recognizing that the child is struggling with sensory overload, and holding them accountable means gently guiding them through their emotional responses without judgment. For example, if a child melts down at a social gathering, a parent might provide support by calmly helping them step away from the crowd, validating their feelings, and offering strategies to calm down. This approach reinforces the idea that while the child's feelings are valid, they are still responsible for managing their behavior.

Courage is crucial here as well. It takes courage to set boundaries with love, especially when the child's reactions are intense. Wisdom helps parents recognize the right time to step in with support and the right time to allow the child to handle the situation independently. Through this balance of compassion and accountability, parents create a stable environment where children feel safe and supported, yet also learn that their actions have consequences, which is an important lesson in developing emotional maturity.

The Role of Consequences and Accountability in Stoic Parenting

The Necessity of Fair Consequences in Parenting

When it comes to parenting children with SPD, one of the most difficult but important aspects is ensuring that fair consequences are applied for their behavior. Stoic philosophy teaches that everything in life has a natural order, and that includes how we respond to actions and behaviors. Children, including those with SPD, need to understand that their actions have consequences—both positive and negative. This concept of justice is vital in the Stoic approach to parenting. Justice isn't about punishment, but about ensuring fairness and balance in how we respond to our children's actions. For children with SPD, who may struggle to control their emotions due to sensory overload, fair consequences help them understand that while their emotional reactions are valid, there are still expectations for their behavior.

Fair consequences create a stable environment in which the child can learn responsibility. For example, if a child reacts strongly to a situation due to sensory overload, it's important for parents to acknowledge the child's struggle while also enforcing clear consequences for any behavior that might negatively impact others. This might mean helping the child to calm down and then discussing the behavior in a constructive way. Parents must be patient and ensure that the consequences are proportional to the situation, allowing the child to learn the lessons without feeling punished for something they cannot fully control. This approach encourages growth, emotional regulation, and ultimately self-discipline.

Wisdom and temperance come into play when applying consequences. Wisdom ensures that parents understand the root cause of the child's behavior and temperance helps them to respond in a measured way. Instead of reacting impulsively, Stoic parents take a step back, evaluate the situation calmly, and decide on a fair consequence that aligns with the child's age, emotional state, and understanding. Through this thoughtful process, children begin to internalize the idea that actions have consequences, and they develop a sense of accountability and responsibility.

Teaching Accountability Without Guilt or Shame

Teaching accountability to children with SPD involves a delicate balance between recognizing the challenges they face and holding them responsible for their actions. It's crucial to remember that guilt and shame are not productive teaching tools. Stoic parenting emphasizes that self-reflection and understanding are the keys to growth, rather than inducing guilt. For children with SPD, feelings of guilt or shame can intensify emotional distress and worsen the situation. Therefore, the goal is not to make the child feel bad about their behavior but to help them understand the impact of their actions and encourage responsibility without judgment.

Accountability comes through honest and compassionate conversation. When a child with SPD has a sensory meltdown, for example, the parent's job is to help the child reflect on their behavior without shaming them. After the child has calmed down, parents can use the moment to discuss how their reaction affected others and what they could do differently next time. Justice is reflected here in how the parent ensures that the child understands that their actions have consequences, but also that they are loved and supported regardless of mistakes. This reinforces the child's self-worth while teaching them that they are responsible for their actions, even when they cannot control their sensory responses entirely.

Courage is needed when a parent consistently teaches accountability in the face of challenging behaviors. It's not always easy to stay calm and focused during a meltdown or difficult situation, but courage allows the parent to stand firm in their approach while maintaining compassion. By modeling courage and patience, parents teach their children that it is okay to make mistakes and learn from them. This process empowers the child to take ownership of their actions and behavior, which helps them grow emotionally and learn how to handle sensory challenges in the future.

The Role of Positive Reinforcement in Teaching Accountability

While consequences are important for teaching accountability, positive reinforcement is equally vital. For children with SPD, reinforcing positive behavior encourages them to continue making progress. In Stoic parenting, justice doesn't just involve holding the child accountable for their mistakes; it also involves recognizing and rewarding their growth and effort. Positive reinforcement helps children with SPD feel recognized for their achievements, no matter how small, and provides the motivation to continue striving for improvement. The key is to offer encouragement in a way that fosters growth without pressure.

For example, when a child successfully handles a sensory challenge—whether it's using a calming technique during a meltdown or simply staying calm in a crowded environment—praise and acknowledgment from the parent reinforces that behavior. This helps the child understand that they have the ability to navigate sensory difficulties and that their efforts are valued. Positive reinforcement is about recognizing the child's strengths and progress rather than focusing solely on the struggles.

Wisdom and temperance are crucial when using positive reinforcement. Wisdom allows parents to recognize which behaviors are worth reinforcing, while temperance helps ensure that praise is given in a balanced way. Over-praising can lead to a sense of entitlement, but when reinforcement is done thoughtfully and genuinely, it encourages the child to continue developing self-discipline and resilience. By consistently reinforcing positive behaviors, parents can help their children build confidence and a sense of responsibility for their own actions.

Using Reflection to Teach Accountability

One of the most powerful tools for teaching accountability is reflection. Stoic philosophy teaches the value of looking back on experiences with a calm and analytical mindset. For children with SPD, this can be especially helpful after a challenging sensory episode. Once the child has calmed down, parents can guide them through a reflective process, asking questions like, "What happened? How did it make you feel? How could we handle that differently next time?" By focusing on reflection rather than punishment, parents help their child gain a deeper understanding of their own behavior and reactions.

Temperance plays a key role in this process. Reflecting on behavior calmly and without judgment allows both the child and the parent to see the situation for what it is—an opportunity for growth. When a parent is patient during the reflection process, the child learns that it's okay to make mistakes, but they are also responsible for learning from them. This process also encourages self-awareness in children, which is a crucial skill for managing sensory overload in the future.

Reflection also provides parents with the chance to assess their own actions. Parenting a child with SPD can be emotionally taxing, and parents must be aware of how their responses may impact the child's behavior. Through reflection, parents can examine what worked, what didn't, and how they can adjust their approach moving forward. This helps parents improve their own emotional regulation and response strategies, making them better equipped to guide their child through future challenges.

Balancing Accountability with Compassion

In the Stoic approach to parenting, it is essential to balance accountability with compassion. While accountability teaches children that they are responsible for their actions, compassion reminds them that their sensory struggles are valid and deserve understanding. This is particularly important for children with SPD, as they may feel misunderstood or frustrated by their inability to control sensory overloads. Compassion means acknowledging that the child's reaction to a sensory event is not intentional but a result of their heightened sensitivities.

By combining justice with compassion, parents can ensure that the child feels both supported and held accountable. For instance, when a child has a sensory meltdown, parents should validate the child's experience—acknowledging how difficult the situation must have been—while also reinforcing the importance of managing behavior in such circumstances. This shows the child that their emotions are valid, but their actions still have consequences, and they are capable of learning new coping mechanisms over time.

In practicing both accountability and compassion, parents help their children develop emotional resilience. By seeing their parents handle their emotional responses with calmness and fairness, children learn that they, too, can manage their emotions in a healthy way. This balance of empathy and responsibility is crucial in raising a child with SPD, as it fosters an environment where the child feels secure enough to explore and learn while understanding the importance of managing their actions.

Pandora's Box

The myth of Pandora's Box is one of the most iconic stories in Greek mythology, often interpreted as a tale about the consequences of unchecked curiosity and the eventual release of unforeseen troubles into the world. Pandora, given a box with explicit instructions not to open it, inevitably succumbs to her curiosity and releases all the evils of the world—pain, sorrow, greed, and strife. However, in the end, when all seemed lost, Pandora discovered that the box also contained hope. This final gift, often interpreted as a glimmer of light amidst the darkness, offers a powerful lesson in the face of adversity.

In many ways, Pandora's Box serves as a reflection of the challenges faced by parents of children with SPD. Much like Pandora's actions, the experience of raising a child with sensory sensitivities can feel as though a box of overwhelming difficulties has been opened. Sensory overload, meltdowns, and emotional difficulties can seem like uncontrollable forces, much like the evils Pandora unleashed. Yet, much like Pandora discovering hope at the bottom of the box, there are moments of clarity and peace that can be found through reflection, understanding, and adaptability. These moments—although sometimes fleeting—serve as powerful reminders that growth, resilience, and understanding are possible, even in the midst of chaos.

For parents practicing Stoic parenting, this myth highlights the importance of virtue, particularly the Stoic virtues of patience, wisdom, and temperance, in handling the overwhelming experiences that can come with SPD. Stoicism teaches us that while we cannot control the external circumstances—such as the sensory stimuli or emotional reactions that may arise—we can control how we respond to these challenges. Just as Pandora's initial action unleashed a storm of negative outcomes, a parent's impulsive or reactive actions can escalate sensory challenges for their child. However, like Pandora's final discovery of hope, a Stoic parent understands that calmness, patience, and reflection can help reframe these moments and guide both the child and parent towards growth.

The virtues of temperance and wisdom are particularly relevant here. In Stoic parenting, temperance is about moderating one's emotional responses and wisdom is about understanding that every difficult moment with a child, especially one with SPD, is an opportunity for growth—for both parent and child. Just as Pandora's box held not just evil but hope, parents can recognize that within the trials of SPD are moments of opportunity. Each meltdown or sensory overload is a chance to practice patience and self-control, both in how we respond and how we guide our child toward better managing their sensory experiences.

Finally, much like Pandora's journey of discovery, Stoic parenting invites us to acknowledge that while life may present difficulties and uncertainties, it is through the practice of virtue—patience, wisdom, and temperance—that we find hope and resilience. Raising a child with SPD can be a journey filled with unexpected moments, some challenging and others deeply rewarding. The myth of Pandora's Box teaches us that by cultivating hope—even amidst the challenges—we can find new strength and clarity, enabling us to better serve our children and ourselves. In Stoic parenting, reflection on these moments, and learning from them, provides the foundation for a more peaceful, understanding, and purposeful approach to parenting a child with sensory sensitivities.

Conclusion

Embracing the Journey – The Endless Dance of Love and Growth

As I sit here, reflecting on the journey we've shared with our son, I am filled with a sense of gratitude that words can scarcely capture. He's funny, caring, playful, and spirited—everything you could want in a child. But more than that, he's uniquely himself, with a world of experiences that are as beautiful as they are challenging. Raising a child with Sensory Processing Disorder (SPD) is a journey that constantly evolves, and though it can feel unpredictable and uncertain, it is also deeply rewarding.

Through the approaches shared in this book, we've learned to move forward with a sense of purpose—a plan of attack, if you will. We've embraced the practices of empathy, self-reflection, patience, and adaptability, and they have transformed the way we support him. But the most important lesson I've learned is this: **Things will work until they don't. And when they don't, it's time to pivot, try again, and evolve your plan with your child.** There's no one-size-fits-all solution. It's an ever-changing dance, where we adjust and readjust, and sometimes, just when we think we've figured something out, we find it no longer works. And that's okay.

What matters most is that we keep moving forward with love and a willingness to change. Our child is growing, and we are growing alongside him. His development is a dynamic, unfolding story—one that we are so privileged to be a part of. The time we spend with him is precious, and though it's not always easy, it's always worth it. Every laugh, every playful moment, and every tiny victory reminds us that the journey is just as important as the destination.

As parents, we have a responsibility to evolve with our child. They grow, change, and develop in ways we can't always predict. Our job is to be flexible, to keep our hearts open, and to adjust our strategies when necessary. Our son has taught us to embrace the journey with humility and grace, and as we adapt to his needs, we're finding joy in the moments, not just the milestones.

I hope that the strategies and perspectives shared in this book offer you a sense of hope, clarity, and understanding—just as they've helped us. More than anything, I hope they help you enjoy the time with your child the way I am lucky enough to enjoy mine. For, at the end of the day, that's what truly matters: the connection, the love, and the laughter we share as we navigate this wild, beautiful journey together.

Remember: things will work until they don't. And that's not a reason to give up; it's simply an invitation to begin again, to try something new, and to continue evolving. With patience, empathy, and a willingness to grow alongside our children, we can face whatever comes next with confidence and love.

www.ingramcontent.com/pod-product-compliance
Lightning Source LLC
Chambersburg PA
CBHW040639100526
44585CB00039B/2823